LEMON SEEDS

SEEDS

When Life Squeezes You
Faith Grows You

NADINE MALDONADO

SHINE
PRESS

Tampa, Florida

Publisher: Shine Press
4522 W. Village Dr. #1294
Tampa, Florida 34624
Shine-Press.com | Jodi@Shine-Press.com
Shine Press is an imprint of Jodi K Costa, LLC.

Disclaimer: This book is a personal account of the author's experiences and perspective. The events, conversations, and situations described are based her life, and while she has made every effort to present them as accurately as possible, they are filtered through her personal lens.

Please note that some names and other identifying details may have been changed to protect the privacy of individuals mentioned in this story.

For speaking engagements, event invitations, bulk orders, and other author requests, please contact her publisher: Jodi@Shine-Press.com

F I R S T   E D I T I O N

ISBN: 979-8-9937924-1-5

Dedication

To Jaylin, Alexa, and Simon

You are the reason I chose to grow instead of break, trust instead of fear, and believe when life didn't make sense. Every chapter of this story has traces of you in it.

My prayer is that you always know God carried us, covered us, and continues to lead us into everything He promised.

You are my greatest purpose,
my greatest joy, and the reason I kept going.

Love you forever & always!

CONTENTS

INTRODUCTION

If you're holding this book, you're probably standing in a place I know all too well. Where you're trying to breathe through disappointment, hold yourself together, and still somehow believe that things can get better.

If that's you… come in. This book was written with you in mind.

I don't know exactly what brought you here, but I know what it feels like to wake up in a season that doesn't look anything like the one you prayed for. I know what it feels like to wonder why certain things happened, why people changed, why doors closed, and why life keeps demanding strength from you when you're already running on empty.

I wrote *Lemon Seeds* because I learned something in the middle of my own breaking:

**You don't have to understand the
season for the seed to grow.**

There were moments I didn't think I'd ever feel whole again. Moments I couldn't see God working but later realized He was holding every piece of my life in His hands. These were the moments where I found strength I didn't even know existed.

This book isn't about my pain. It's about what came after. It's about the seeds that were planted in the very moments I thought I was falling apart.

My prayer is that as you read these pages, you feel less alone.
That something in you softens.
That hope rises.
That you begin to see your story through a different lens, one where even the hardest parts still hold purpose.

You don't have to have it all figured out.
You don't have to be fully healed yet.
You don't even have to feel strong today.
You just have to be willing to keep going.

So take a deep breath, settle in, and let's walk through this together, one seed at a time.

~ One ~

SOUR BEGINNINGS

If we think about how God intended our creation, it was never accidental, it was fully intentional. God formed us in His image, which means we were created with the ability to love deeply, create boldly, endure hardship, rebuild again, and rise when life tries to bring us low. He knew everything about us before we ever took a breath. Jeremiah 1:5 tells us, "Before I formed you, I knew you." To me, that means before any pain, heartbreak, or loss ever entered my story, God had already woven purpose into my existence.

Even knowing that God created us with intention, most of us reach a point where life doesn't feel intentional at all. We step into seasons that shake us, stretch us, and squeeze us in ways we never saw coming. The purpose God placed inside us can feel distant when we're standing in the middle of a beginning that tastes sour. Sour beginnings aren't new, even the strongest, most faithful people in Scripture walked through them. Job is one of them. He was a man known for his faith, integrity, and devotion to God… yet his life shifted in a moment, and everything that once felt secure suddenly fell apart. He didn't understand why. He didn't see it

9

coming. He didn't feel prepared. In many ways, I relate to that, because there came a moment in my own life where everything I thought was stable was stripped down to the foundation.

It feels like the end of everything you once knew. The plans, dreams, and assumptions about your life dissolve in an instant. Time feels distorted; the days stretch endlessly, and the nights are even longer. You might find yourself moving through life in a haze, unable to connect to the world around you. Frozen in your hurt, consumed by the rawness of your pain, it can feel as though life has abandoned you.

In the moments that feel like total destruction, God is doing something we can't yet see. The enemy has a way of convincing us that everything is falling apart, when in reality, something is being rebuilt beneath the surface. Just like Job, we're not always given answers at the moment. We're not handed explanations or timelines. What we are given, though, is the quiet presence of a God who stays near, even when we feel numb, unseen, or forgotten. Looking back, I didn't realize that my sour beginning wasn't meant to destroy me. It was meant to uncover me, to strip away the life I had outgrown and guide me into the life God was trying to lead me toward.

For me, that uncovering began slowly at first. Little shifts I brushed off. Quiet discomforts I tried to ignore. Moments where something inside me whispered that the life I was living no longer fit the woman I was becoming. I didn't want to admit it, not to myself, not to anyone. So I kept moving, kept trying, kept holding everything together. Eventually, the cracks I ignored became too deep to hide. The life I thought was secure, the future I planned, the identity I built… it all began to slip through my hands. What I didn't know then was that this was the beginning of my sour season — the moment where everything familiar would break open and force me into a place I never expected to be.

 LEMON SEEDS

There is a worship song called Something Has To Break by Red Rock Worship & Essential Worship, and I encourage you to pause your reading for a moment and turn on this song. They sing, "I believe you will lead me through it, I believe you'll get me to it, I believe you will do it right now, Something has to break" in this song they sing about how God will keep working to get us closer to Him, to get us to freedom, and breaking off everything in our lives that is not meant from God.

What if our pain isn't proof that God has left us, but evidence that He is doing a deeper work within us? What if the breaking is actually the beginning of becoming? I've learned that God often allows the things we cling to the tightest to fall away, not to hurt us, but to free us. Sometimes what we call heartbreak is really His protection. Sometimes what feels like the end is His way of removing the weight we were never meant to carry. Sometimes the bitter moments are the very places where God gently separates us from the identities, relationships, expectations, and versions of ourselves that were never aligned with who He created us to be. Pain doesn't just take things from us, it reveals what was never meant to stay.

I didn't understand any of this when my own breaking began. All I could see was what I was losing, not what God might be clearing space for. Like most of us, I tried to hold on. I tried to fix what was unraveling and force what was fading to stay. There comes a moment when life makes it impossible to keep pretending. A moment when the squeeze becomes too strong to ignore. A moment when God allows something so deep, so painful, so unexpected, that it changes the way you see everything, including yourself. For me, that moment came long before I had the language for it.

I remember the first time I felt completely broken. I was 20 years old and the mother of a beautiful one-year-old girl named Jaylin. I got pregnant with Jaylin at 19 years old, from a man I later married and spent 15 years of my life with. I remember telling my mom, "You're going to have to stay with me and teach me this whole mom thing." The moment Jaylin was born, something clicked. Being her mom came so naturally. It was as if I'd been born for it.

Before Jaylin, I didn't feel like I was particularly great at anything. Motherhood was different, it gave me purpose. My entire life became about her. Every decision I made was for her, and I lived and breathed to be the best mom I could be. To me being the best mom I could be meant more than just nurturing and caring, it meant capturing and soaking up every moment we had together. In Jaylin's first year of life we did everything together, mommy daughter road trips, family trips to Disney World and our favorite historic city St. Augustine. We did beach days, baseball games, endless shopping trips, we were Hannah Montana fans. She would sit on my lap while I tried to finish my college classes, and occasionally would crawl into the room and press the power button as I was finishing a 2500 word essay. The amount of pictures I captured during those moments were endless, they still bring so much joy to me today.

One night, everything changed in an instant. Her father and I were headed out to dinner, planning to drop Jaylin off at her grandparents' house first. We were listening to music, laughing, and talking about nothing important at all, just the normal rhythm of life. Jaylin was in the backseat asking for her teddy. Then, without warning, life split into a before and an after.

The crash was sudden. The world went silent. What I remember most is the confusion, the stillness, and the terror of not being able to reach my daughter. I remained conscious, but everything around me felt far away, voices, movement, people rushing toward us, all I could think about was Jaylin. I kept calling out for her, praying someone would tell me she was okay.

LEMON SEEDS

At the hospital, I begged the doctors to let me be with her, but my injuries required immediate surgery. The next time I opened my eyes, I awoke to a reality no mother should ever have to face. Jaylin's injuries were too severe. There was nothing more they could do.

We had to make an impossible decision. My mind raced with memories of her laugh, her first birthday we had just celebrated, our road trips, the extra time I rearranged in my life to spend with her. Nothing prepared me for that moment.

In the days that followed, I questioned everything about my faith, my purpose, my strength, even my will to keep going. Grief came in waves I didn't know how to survive. I felt betrayed by life, abandoned by the future I thought I had, and crushed under the weight of a pain so deep it didn't feel human.

Even in that darkness, something quietly shifted inside me. I didn't see it then, and I didn't feel it, but looking back, I can recognize the moment God began His rebuilding. It wasn't strength, not yet. It was awareness. A sensitivity. A deeper knowing that life would never look the same, and neither would I. Losing Jaylin didn't just break me, it awakened something in me. It peeled back layers I didn't know I had, exposed parts of my heart I had never faced, and forced me to meet a version of myself I had never been introduced to. This was the first sour beginning the one that would shape every season that followed, the one that planted the early seeds of the woman I would one day become

In many ways, I found myself standing in a place Job once stood, a place where nothing made sense and everything hurt. Job suffered immense losses of wealth, children, and health. He knew what it meant to wake up to a life he didn't recognize, to have the world he trusted suddenly collapse beneath him. He knew what it felt like to question everything, to sit in the silence and wonder where God was in all the pain.

Job was a man of unwavering faith. Even in his grief, he never denied God. I wish I could say the same about myself, but when I lost Jaylin, my faith didn't hold. It shattered. I wanted nothing to do with God. I pushed Him away. I didn't believe, I didn't trust, and I didn't understand how a God who claimed to love me could let something so devastating happen to me.

Losing my faith didn't happen in a dramatic moment, it happened in the quiet, heavy places where grief made it hard to breathe. I wasn't just angry with God at first; I was wounded by Him. I felt abandoned, singled out, and forgotten. I didn't want Scripture, encouragement, or anyone telling me, "God has a plan." I didn't want a plan. I wanted my daughter. When I couldn't have her, something inside me closed. I didn't realize it then, but that was the moment my heart hardened in ways I wouldn't understand until years later. I wasn't rejecting God as much as I was trying to protect myself from more pain. What I couldn't see was that even when I wanted nothing to do with Him, He never stopped pursuing me.

Scripture tells us, "The Lord is near to the brokenhearted and saves those who are crushed in spirit" (Psalm 34:18). I couldn't feel His nearness. All I felt was the crushing. I couldn't feel His presence, but that didn't mean He wasn't there.

Even though I pushed God away, something quiet was happening beneath the surface, something I couldn't see or name at the time. Losing Jaylin planted the earliest seeds of the woman I would one day become. It awakened a depth in me I didn't know existed. It made me see life differently, love differently, and hold onto people differently. It made me more aware, more empathetic, more present. Pain has a way of reshaping you long before you realize you've changed. That loss became a defining marker in my story, not because of what it took from me, but because of what it eventually built within me. Even in the bitterness of that season, God was sowing something sacred in the dark, something that would grow later, long after I thought my life was over.

Healing begins with acceptance, not the kind of acceptance that makes you okay with what happened, but the kind that acknowledges reality without fighting it. You don't have to like it, agree with it, or understand it to begin moving through it. Acceptance is simply the moment you stop resisting what is, so you can breathe again.

Weeks after losing Jaylin, I returned home to a house that felt unbearably silent, yet constantly full of people. Visitors came daily, offering condolences, prayers, meals, and the kind of well-meaning words that I had no capacity to absorb. At the time, I didn't want any of it. I didn't want sympathy. I didn't want people telling me they were sorry or that they understood. Because how could they? Looking back now, though, I see the beauty in their presence. Even in my numbness, even when I couldn't receive their comfort, they still showed up. Now, with time and perspective, I'm deeply grateful for every single person who stood in the gap for me when I had nothing left to give.

One day, a friend's mother, Terry, came by. She handed me a small gift: a journal with a set of beautiful metallic pens.

"Use this when you feel like you need it," she said gently. "Write down how you're feeling. It will help."

At first, I smiled politely, thanking her for the gift, inwardly I felt numb. In those days, it was hard to feel anything beyond the crushing weight of grief. To be honest, I was more excited about the metallic pens than the journal. They were the brightest thing in my life, and their shimmer was almost mocking amidst the dullness of my days. I didn't know then that this small gesture, this simple journal would become my lifeline.

WRITING THROUGH THE PAIN

I couldn't do much in those early days. My injuries from the accident left me bedridden and completely dependent on others. My amazing mother stepped in with the kind of strength only mothers have. She helped me with everything, tasks I had taken for granted just weeks before. I spent most of my days lying in bed, staring at the ceiling, crying, and wishing I could wake up from the nightmare my life had become. My body was healing, but my spirit felt shattered beyond repair.

Then one day, out of desperation… or maybe curiosity… I reached for one of those metallic pens and opened the journal Terry had given me. The blank pages stared back at me, almost inviting me to place my pain somewhere outside of myself. So I began to write.

I didn't have answers for what I was feeling. I only knew I couldn't hold it in anymore. I wrote about my anger, my confusion, my heartbreak. I wrote the questions that felt too heavy to speak out loud. How did my life change in the blink of an eye? What had I done to deserve this? Why would God allow something so devastating to happen?

The words poured out of me like a flood raw, unfiltered, and heavy. I didn't try to make it poetic or presentable. I didn't try to protect God or myself from the honesty of my grief. I was angry. Angry at God. Angry at the person who caused the accident. Angry at the medical team who couldn't save her. Angry at myself, replaying the moment over and over, wondering why I couldn't get to Jaylin when she needed me most.

That journal became the only place where I let myself pour it all out. Page after page held the pieces of me I couldn't show anyone else. If tears could stain through paper, those pages would have been washed away. It was the one space where I didn't have to be strong, composed, or brave. I could simply be broken.

 LEMON SEEDS

THE BURDEN OF STRENGTH

I felt an unspoken obligation to hold everything together. I believed that if I smiled, others would smile. If I stayed strong, it would help everyone else feel strong too. I didn't understand how heavy that expectation was until much later.

During one of my early therapy sessions, my therapist asked a question that stopped me cold. "How can you be strong for others when you are weak?"

I answered without thinking, "Because if I'm strong, then no one has to worry about me."

She looked at me with a gentleness I wasn't prepared for and said, "So you don't feel like you are worthy of being worried about?"

I froze. "Well… no—yes—no. People worry about me. I just don't know how to let them in."

She leaned forward and said words that cut through every wall I had built: "Nadine, you have to be okay with being weak. You are human. You just buried your daughter. Your body is still healing. You need someone to lean on. From the looks of the waiting room, you have a support system."

Her words shook me. I wish I could tell you that everything changed in that moment, but it didn't. It took years, nearly fifteen, for me to truly understand what she meant, and something I work towards until this day. Strength had become my survival mode. Weakness felt unsafe. Letting people in felt impossible. It would take time, life, more breaking, and more rebuilding for me to realize that strength was never meant to be my only identity.

2 Corinthians 12:9 says, "My grace is sufficient for you, for My power is made perfect in weakness." This verse is God literally saying, "you don't have to be strong for me to move. I do my best work when you stop trying to hold everything alone!"

THE DISTRACTION OF AVOIDANCE

For a long time, I believed I was healing simply because I was functional. I could wake up, go to physical therapy, plaster on a brave face, and even support other people through their problems. I was the friend who listened, the daughter who smiled, the one everyone pointed to and said, "She's so strong." The truth was, I wasn't okay. I wasn't anywhere close to okay.

I was surviving, not healing. I moved through my days like a shell of myself, present on the outside, unraveling on the inside. Everything I did was held together by a thin thread of strength that wasn't really strength at all. It was fear. Fear of falling apart. Fear of being seen. Fear of being too much or not enough.

I remember one day that cracked my mask wide open. My mom and I had just come home from physical therapy, and I felt defeated in every sense of the word. I sat in my wheelchair in the living room, surrounded by a wall of decorative vases. Something in me snapped. I broke down crying in front of her raw, exposed, vulnerable in a way that terrified me. When my mom's eyes filled with worry, guilt washed over me. I hated that she saw my pain. I hated that I caused her more hurt. In my frustration, I reached for a vase and threw it across the room. It shattered against the wall, echoing everything I felt inside.

The moment the pieces hit the floor, I panicked. I forced out a laugh and said, "I must have needed that. I'm alright now." But I wasn't. I was anything but. The second I saw her face, I retreated again. I put the mask

　　　　　　LEMON SEEDS

back on. I hid the messy, hurting parts of me because I didn't know how to let anyone carry them with me.

Focusing on everyone else became my escape. It was easier to take care of people than to sit with my own grief, anger, and guilt. Looking back, I can see how deeply I mistook distraction for strength. I convinced myself that if I could just stay busy enough, helpful enough, needed enough, I wouldn't have to confront what was breaking me.

I know I'm not alone in this. Avoidance is a human coping mechanism. We bury ourselves in work, relationships, distractions, and endless to-do lists because facing our pain feels too overwhelming. Avoidance isn't healing. It's a bandage placed over a wound that desperately needs to be cleaned. Until we face what hurts, we can't heal from what broke us.

WHY WE AVOID

Avoidance can take many forms. For some, it looks like staying endlessly busy, burying yourself in work, social commitments, or even caretaking for everyone around you. For others, it shows up in numbing, turning to substances, mindless scrolling, or binge-watching anything that keeps you from sitting in silence.

At its core, avoidance is fear. Fear of what we might uncover if we slow down long enough to feel. Fear of being swallowed by the pain. Fear of losing control. Fear of acknowledging truths we've spent years trying to outrun. Avoidance convinces us that as long as we stay moving, we'll stay safe. The reality is, we're not avoiding the pain… we're avoiding the healing.

Journaling became my way of gently peeling back the layers of avoidance. It didn't demand that I face everything all at once. It allowed me to move at my own pace, to release only what my heart had the capacity to hold in that moment. Some days, I could only scribble a sentence or two. Even those small, shaky attempts at honesty were steps forward. Steps toward myself. Steps toward my healing.

JOURNALING: FACING THE PAIN

The journal from Terry became the one place I couldn't hide. On those pages, I couldn't distract myself with someone else's problems or sweep my emotions under the rug. I had to face them.

When I wrote, there were no masks, no brave faces, no distractions, just raw, unfiltered honesty. I could pour out every dark thought, every ounce of anger, every tear I had been holding back. The surprising thing was this: the more I wrote, the lighter I began to feel.

That journal became the place where I stopped pretending. It taught me how to sit with my pain instead of running from it. It forced me to acknowledge the depth of my grief and the toll it was taking on me. In the beginning, it felt excruciating. Writing about my pain made it feel real in a way I wasn't ready for. Slowly, journaling became more than an outlet, it became a mirror. A tool for self-discovery.

As I wrote, patterns began to reveal themselves. I started to see the ways I was avoiding my feelings and distracting myself with the needs of others. I began to recognize the walls I had built, the ways I hid behind strength, and the truths I had been too afraid to admit.

TAKE ROOT

If you tend to avoid your feelings by pouring into others or staying busy, journaling can help you finally face your pain. It gives you space to slow down, to tell the truth, and to meet yourself honestly. Here's how you can use it to gently break the cycle of avoidance.

   LEMON SEEDS

1. Start Small

You don't have to write pages at a time. Begin with a single sentence about how you're feeling at that moment.

Prompt: "Right now, I feel __ because __."

2. Be Honest

Let your journal be a judgment-free zone. Write down your rawest, most unfiltered thoughts, even if they are messy or contradictory.

Prompt: "What am I avoiding right now? Why am I avoiding it?"

3. Reflect on Your Patterns

Occasionally , look back at what you've written. Are there recurring themes or feelings? Are there areas of your life where you're consistently avoiding something?

Prompt: "What patterns do I notice in how I handle pain or conflict?"

4. Ask Yourself Questions

Use your journal to dig deeper into your emotions.

Examples:

> "What am I afraid will happen if I face this pain head-on?"
>
> "What would it look like to give myself permission to feel every thing, even if it hurts?"

5. Write Letters You'll Never Send

If your pain involves other people, try writing letters to them. Say everything you wish you could say, even if it's angry, hurtful, or incomplete. These letters are for your eyes only.

HEALING THROUGH HONESTY

Avoidance might feel easier in the moment, but it always comes with a cost. The pain you bury doesn't disappear, it waits. It lingers beneath the surface and finds its way out in unexpected forms: anxiety that tightens your chest, anger that erupts sideways, or a quiet emptiness you can't explain.

The moment you choose to face your pain the moment you write it down and call it what it is you begin the process of healing.

You stop pretending it doesn't exist.
You stop minimizing what hurt you.
You stop acting like it didn't break your heart.

Instead, you tell the truth:

This person hurt me, and I feel betrayed.
This situation scared me, and now I feel unsafe.
I didn't like how that was handled, and now I feel unseen.

When you put a name to your pain, you take away its power to control you in the shadows.
The silence that once protected your wounds becomes the very thing that suffocates your healing. But when you speak it, when you call it what it is, you bring it into the light.

The light is where God does His best work.

You stop being a prisoner to the things you never voiced.
You stop carrying shame for feelings you were never meant to bury.
You stop living as a half-version of yourself, weighed down by the things you refuse to face.

This is where healing begins.
Not in the pretending.
Not in the performing.
But in the soul-deep, sacred honesty that says:

This is what happened.
This is how it made me feel.
I'm not burying it anymore.

That kind of honesty cracks open the parts of you that have been holding everything together for far too long and it makes room for something new.
Something whole.
Something holy.

Because the truth doesn't just set you free… it brings you home.

Journaling taught me that it's normal to feel everything.
It's okay to break.
It's okay not to have the answers.
It's okay to be human.

Piece by piece, word by word, I began stitching myself back together.

Pick up the pen. Start writing.
Even if the words don't come easily.
Even if it feels strange or uncomfortable.
Keep going. You can't outrun your pain but you can face it.
When you do, that's where healing begins.

SEED FOR THOUGHT

Being broken doesn't mean you're unfixable. It means you've been given the chance to rebuild stronger, softer, wiser, and more beautifully than before. The cracks in your heart aren't flaws. They are the places where the light of God shines through.

"He heals the brokenhearted
and binds up their wounds."

Psalm 147:3

 LEMON SEEDS

Two

BITTER ROOTS

Pain has a way of bringing us face-to-face with some of life's toughest questions. When we're in the midst of heartbreak, loss, or grief, one question rises louder than the rest: *Why me?*

It's a question born from our need to make sense of suffering. As humans, we're wired to connect the dots, to search for meaning in the chaos, and to hope there's some purpose behind the pain we're forced to carry. When life feels unfair, we ask these questions not because we're weak… but because we're desperate for hope. Desperate for something to hold on to when everything else feels lost.

In the early days after losing my daughter, Jaylin, "Why me?" echoed in my mind on repeat.

What had I done to deserve this?
Why did this happen to my little girl?
Was I being punished?

I replayed every part of my life, digging for reasons, searching for answers that never came.

I thought about mistakes I made as a child and in my troubled teen years. The summer I stole my parents' car and drove around all night like I was invincible. The countless days I skipped school. The moments I disobeyed my parents and gave them more worry than any daughter should.

Was this payback for being a reckless teenager?

Then I thought about the less-than-perfect moments I had as a young mom the times I lost patience, raised my voice, or felt overwhelmed. Did those moments deem me unfit to be her mother? Was God taking away the only thing that gave me purpose?

Why me? Why her? Why us?

These were the questions that churned in my soul questions soaked in guilt, confusion, and pain.

Here's what I eventually learned, and what I want you to know too:

None of those reasons are why I experienced one of the greatest losses a person can face. Not the mistakes. Not the imperfections. Not the human moments we all wish we could redo.

God doesn't operate out of punishment. He doesn't keep score. He doesn't take from us to teach us lessons.

Lamentations 3:33 reminds us God is not a punisher, God is not cruel, God does not delight in your suffering. "For He does not willingly bring affliction or grief to anyone."

That truth alone dismantles the lie that I somehow deserved the pain I walked through.

 LEMON SEEDS

Sometimes, life doesn't give us answers. Sometimes, we don't get to know why. In the absence of "Why me?" God invites us into a deeper, more transformational question:

"What can this teach me?"

THE "WHY ME?" TWIST

Shifting from "why me?" to "what can this teach me?" doesn't happen overnight. It's not about ignoring your pain, pretending to be okay, or forcing yourself into a positivity you don't feel. It's about gradually opening your heart to the possibility that, as senseless as your suffering may seem, it holds lessons that can shape you in ways comfort never could.

After losing Jaylin, I wrestled with this shift.

In the beginning, I denied God's goodness. I denied His love. I denied any idea that He was for me. I felt abandoned and left to pick up the pieces alone, so I convinced myself that if I was ever going to feel whole again, it was entirely up to me. I will dive deeper as to why this was the perfect route to destruction in later chapters.

Slowly, almost imperceptibly at first, glimmers of meaning began to show themselves within my grief. A deeper appreciation for time with loved ones. A clearer understanding of what truly matters. The realization that Jaylin's short life taught me more about unconditional love than anything I had ever experienced.

Her absence revealed a resilience I didn't know I had. Her life awakened something sacred in me. Her love became one of the greatest teachers I would ever know.

A dear friend and my first mentor, Katia, once said something to me that I carry with me to this day. She told me:

"How beautiful is it that you get to feel this human emotion in this life journey?"

At first, her words stung. It felt like she was telling me to be grateful for the pain of losing my daughter grateful for heartbreak, grateful for suffering.

When you're hurting, even a helping hand can feel like a personal attack. As I sat with her words, I began to understand what she really meant:

How beautiful is it that you experienced a love so profound? Out of all the mothers in the world, I was chosen to be Jaylin's mommy. I got to experience a bond so deep, a love so unconditional, a joy so pure. I had a year filled with more than a thousand pictures each one a gift, each one a reminder of the life she brought into mine.

When we are in pain, it's easy to focus only on what we've lost. The memories that once made us smile become bittersweet, overshadowed by heartbreak.

What if, instead of dwelling only on the absence, we also honor the beauty of the story we lived?

The reason it hurts so deeply is because it was extraordinary. It was meaningful. It was real.

I want to challenge you to think about the moments in your life that brought you joy, love, and purpose even if they're now wrapped in grief. Write them down. Remember them. Treasure them. They are reminders of what made you feel alive.

When I began asking "What can this teach me?" instead of "Why me?", everything shifted. It didn't erase the grief. It didn't make the loss less real. It allowed me to carry it differently.

 LEMON SEEDS

Instead of being consumed by the weight of my sorrow, I began using that weight to build something within me. The pain didn't disappear, it transformed. It became a bridge to understanding, resilience, and a deeper appreciation for the fragile beauty of life.

While the pain remains a part of me, it no longer defines me. It has become a teacher. A compass. A seed that grew into strength I never knew I had.

FINDING MEANING IN ADVERSITY

Throughout my journey, I've found encouragement from others who have walked through similar valleys. One of those people is Lysa TerKeurst, a Christian author and speaker whose honesty and vulnerability have reached millions. Reading her books or listening to her speak felt like looking into a mirror. Her words echoed the heartbreak, disappointment, and healing I've endured, and for the first time, I felt seen in my pain. It's the same connection I pray you feel as you read this book.

Lysa shares her life with a level of authenticity that many people would shy away from. She has faced heartbreaks that could've easily made her retreat from the world. Instead of letting her pain define her, she invited God into the center of it and allowed Him to transform her suffering into purpose. Through her honesty and obedience, she became one of the most influential Christian authors of our time, earning the distinction of a #1 New York Times bestselling author.

Like Lysa, I've come to understand that we hold the power to transform our most heartbreaking moments into opportunities for growth, not just for ourselves, but for also for others. Sharing our stories, even the raw, messy, and imperfect ones, can be profoundly healing. I often imagine the emotional weight Lysa carries when she steps on stage or writes intimate words to her readers. I also imagine the freedom she feels knowing her pain is being used to set someone else free.

This doesn't mean the pain magically disappears. It doesn't mean the loss becomes easier to accept. When we shift our perspective from *"Why is this happening to me?"* to *"This is happening for me,"* something begins to change inside us. We stop seeing our suffering as evidence of God's absence and start seeing it as a doorway to growth.

It's human to feel shattered. It's normal to sit in your grief. To cry. To question. Even in those moments, cling to hope. Healing exists beyond the heartache. Growth emerges from the struggle. Strength is formed in the breaking.

When God's hand is in the midst of your suffering, you can trust that you'll come out on the other side renewed, restored, and redirected. The journey may require effort, tears, honesty, and courage… but it will never be in vain.

TAKE ROOT

If you're struggling to find meaning in your pain, here are some steps to help you begin the process:

1. Reflect on Your Journey

Take some time to journal about what you've been through. Ask yourself, *What have I learned about myself through this experience? How has this changed the way I view life?*

2. Look for Moments of Growth

Think about the ways your pain has shaped you. Have you become more compassionate, resilient, or patient? Sometimes, even the smallest shifts in perspective can reveal meaning.

 LEMON SEEDS

3. Seek Stories of Resilience

Read or listen to the stories of others who have faced adversity and come out stronger. Their experiences can offer comfort and remind you that you're not alone.

4. Focus on Giving Back

One of the most powerful ways to find meaning is to use your pain to help others. Consider volunteering, mentoring, or simply sharing your story with someone who might benefit from your perspective.

SEED FOR THOUGHT

The search for meaning in pain isn't about erasing what happened or pretending it doesn't hurt. It's about recognizing that even in our darkest moments, there is the potential for growth, transformation, and purpose.

When you're ready, please ask yourself: *What can this teach me?* The answer may not come right away, in time, you'll find it and when you do, it will light the way forward.

God wastes nothing.

Not your sorrow.

Not your confusion.

Not a single tear.

**"And we know that in all things God works
for the good of those who love Him, who have
been called according to His purpose"**

Romans 8:28

Three

PULLING THE WEEDS

Life can feel like a relentless effort to hold everything together. We plan, prepare, and grip tightly to the illusion of control, believing that if we do everything "right," life will reward us with smooth sailing. What happens when the storms come anyway? What happens when life reminds us, in the most jarring ways, that control was never really in our hands to begin with?

I wish I could say that after losing my daughter, I never experienced pain again and that surviving such a devastating heartbreak somehow exempted me from future suffering.

That's not how life works. The truth is: pain keeps coming… and so do the lessons it brings.

After Jaylin's passing, I clung tighter to everything that mattered to me. I believed her death meant her father and I had to stay together, no matter what. When Alexa and Simon were born, I became obsessed with protecting them, hovering over every moment as if vigilance alone could prevent tragedy. I convinced myself that if I stayed in a secure corporate job, we would be financially safe. My mindset was simple and rigid:

If I did A, then B had to follow. If I controlled enough, nothing would collapse again.

Life doesn't cooperate with our formulas.

When we're young, we're taught the "safe path":
Go to school.
    Get a degree.
        Secure a job.
            Get married.
                Have kids.
                    Retire peacefully.

Nowhere in that path do they teach us how to survive heartbreak.
Where was the class on grief?
Where was the manual for trauma?
Where was the chapter on rebuilding when life breaks you open?

There is no textbook for navigating devastation. There is only lived experience… and the God who meets us in it.

After losing Jaylin, I pushed Him away and decided everything was up to me. I took full responsibility for outcomes He never asked me to carry. My ego led the way, and I carried the weight of the world on my shoulders. I stayed in situations far longer than I should have, clinging to the illusion of safety, believing that holding tightly would protect me from ever breaking again.

The truth is: my fear covered up more fear.

When we lose a key attachment such as a child, a spouse, or a parent, our nervous system panics. We're wired for connection, so when that bond is suddenly cut, the brain scrambles to feel safe again.

That's when anxious attachment behaviors often show up: codependency, people-pleasing, over-apologizing, over-functioning. We become desperate to prevent any further abandonment. We hold on to everything and everyone, afraid that one more loss might break us completely.

That is exactly where I found myself, caught between fear, survival mode, and a misplaced sense of self-reliance.

THE TURNING POINT

It was 2017 when I started my first business, it was an online venture I worked part-time alongside my full time job. Eventually, craving freedom, I quit my corporate gig far earlier than I should have, convinced that sheer determination would guarantee success.

I turned the online business into a café-style brick-and-mortar shop, something I never imagined for myself. My ego soared. I would tell myself, "After everything I've been through, look at me now!" Pride can set the stage for a fall. During the buildout process, my business partners and I ran out of money.

I had no resources to request assistance from the bank. My ego wouldn't allow me to admit I was in over my head. Roadblock after roadblock piled up, and the pressure became suffocating. Everyone around me kept saying, "Give it to God. He's got this." But instead of comfort, those words felt hollow. My faith didn't run that deep anymore. Somewhere along the way, I had come to believe that God wasn't going to reach for me—that whatever help He offered was meant for people stronger, steadier, and more deserving than I felt.

One day, driving home from the storefront, I finally broke down and prayed out loud:

> *"Okay, God. They say everything is guided by You. I'm still angry with You, and I don't fully trust You, if You brought me here, it wasn't to let me fail before I even started. Even if it was, it wouldn't surprise me because I don't think You like me very much anyway. You see what's happening, my husband is stressed, my business partners are exhausted, and I just want to open this place and make it work. So, God, I give this to You. I give you full control. If You put me here, it's for a reason. Show me what that is."*

That was one of three prayers in my life where I felt God respond almost immediately. The next day, my business partner came into some unexpected money, my brother offered financial help, and the pieces started falling into place. That prayer was the start of daily conversations with God.

JOY IN THE JOURNEY

We opened the café with excitement buzzing in the air. I was the first to walk through the doors of that brand-new space, standing there with my husband and our business partners, hopeful and wide-eyed.

Every single day I walked into that café, I prayed the same simple prayer:

"Let's have a great day. Fill this place with the people who are meant to be here. Allow me to serve others not just their tummies, but their hearts."

I wish I could tell you I made record-breaking sales or became a millionaire. The truth is better… because it's real.

　　　　　LEMON SEEDS

Most days, I barely broke even. Yet my heart was full, overflowing because of the people who walked through those doors.

God used that season to teach me about joy… not the kind the world promises, but the kind He plants deep inside you.

As humans, we chase happiness, something that rises and falls with our circumstances. Happiness is fragile.

God promises joy, something steady, rooted, and unshakable…a quiet strength that grows even when life is hard. As Scripture says:

"You will show me the path of life; in Your presence is fullness of joy; at Your right hand are pleasures forevermore." Psalm 16:11

Don't worry. We'll discuss that seemingly hard-to-achieve JOY in a later chapter.

I remember my then-husband asking me, "How are you so happy when you didn't make any money today?"

My answer never changed: "Because of the people I met."

Joy wasn't coming from my bank account. It was coming from purpose.

One day, a woman sat across from me and opened up about her struggles and we had a breakthrough moment that felt God-orchestrated.

Another time, someone came in discouraged and told me my smile lifted their spirit.

Then, there was the writer who chose our café as her workspace while she finished her book… the same woman who is now the publisher of this book you're holding.

That café didn't make me rich, but it made me deeper. It expanded my heart. It taught me how to show up for people again. It softened the walls around me. It reshaped my faith. It planted seeds in me that I didn't understand until years later.

THE BIGGER PICTURE

God never promised to check off my to-do list or guarantee financial success. What He did promise was joy, peace, and hope, just like Romans 15:13 declares.

I wasn't consumed by the fact that I was barely making minimum wage. I wasn't overwhelmed by the endless tasks or the long hours. I was consumed by the blessings God kept placing in my path, the people He sent, the conversations He orchestrated, the moments of connection that reminded me He was still working, even when my circumstances didn't look "successful."

Letting go of control over the very thing I had prayed for before opening the café didn't mean I was lazy or irresponsible. It meant I was finally trusting that God's plan was better than my own.

When I loosened my grip on the life I was trying so hard to build, I made space for Him to move. What He gave me in return was far greater than anything I could have forced, planned, or orchestrated on my own.

Surrendering control is scary. It's also freeing.

It doesn't mean life will be perfect. It means you stop carrying weight God never asked you to hold.

Trust that even in the chaos, He is working for your good. Trust that joy is possible even in the most unexpected places.

KILLING YOUR EGO

I want to introduce you to something that has the power to lift a weight off your shoulders, a weight you were never meant to carry. Something that frees you from the exhausting pressure of always needing to have the answers, to fix everything, to keep it all together. It's the moment you decide to kill your ego.

Ego doesn't always look like arrogance.
Sometimes it looks like control…
like perfectionism…
like the desperate need to manage how everything unfolds because somewhere deep inside, you believe that if you don't hold it all together, everything will fall apart.

When we cling to control, we take responsibility for every outcome. Every reaction. Every success. Every failure. We shoulder a weight that was never ours to carry, and slowly, it crushes us.

The ego whispers,
"If I don't do it, no one will."
"I have to fix it."
"I have to prove myself."
"I have to be strong all the time."

Hear me clearly… God never asked you to be your own Savior. He asked you to trust Him.

Psalm 37:5 says, "Commit your way to the Lord; trust in Him, and He will act."

Killing your ego means releasing the illusion that you are responsible for everyone's healing, everyone's happiness, and even your own timeline. It means letting go of the need to be right, to be seen a certain way, to be perfect. It means learning to breathe again and letting yourself believe the truth that you are not behind, you are not failing, and nothing about your life is wasted.

The version of you that is trying to survive everything alone is not the real you. That is the version built in survival mode. When you let go of ego, you stop operating from your wounds and start operating from your soul.

From that place, healing comes quicker. Peace finds you easier. Your heart feels lighter. Your mind becomes clearer.

Surrender is not weakness. It is wisdom. Killing your ego is not death, it is resurrection.

I felt this deeply in my business. There were so many days where I felt alone like I was the only one worrying about inventory, recipes, cleaning, managing customers, and keeping the café standing. When things were going well, I took all the credit. When things weren't, I took all the blame.

When I asked God for help not just in a crisis, but daily something shifted. My prayers weren't just pleas for support. They were invitations for Him to walk with me. He became my closest confidant. On days when I couldn't talk to my partners or even trust my own judgment, I turned to Him.

Here's what I discovered:

When I placed the burden on God, I finally allowed myself to work from purpose instead of pressure. Passion instead of fear. Love instead of ego.

Maybe your story isn't about a business. Maybe it's your marriage.
Your kids.   Your job.   Your finances.
          Your friendships.   Your identity.

          LEMON SEEDS

Maybe you're carrying something heavy and thinking, "It's on me. All of it is on me." What a potentially dangerous mindset to adopt.

It feels great to take the glory when things are going right. What about when things get hard when the situation doesn't go in your favor? How do you talk to yourself then?

I truly believe this is why so many people spiral into depression, sadness, panic, or emotional collapse. They've taken on too much responsibility, too much pressure, too many expectations. They lose control of the situation and turn that frustration inward.

They begin to believe lies:
"I'm not enough."
"I failed."
"I should have done more."

Then the labels start piling on, like bricks on their chest. Listen to this, my friend:

You were never meant to carry that weight alone. Not one ounce of it.

When you let go of your ego and allow God to step in and do what only He can do, you free yourself to fully experience the blessings in front of you. Imagine praying for a business, a relationship, or a family, only to become overwhelmed once you get it. Suddenly, you find yourself complaining about the very things you once prayed for.

Take a moment to reflect we've all had one, three, or ten times in our lives when we mishandled our blessings. I believe we confuse God when that happens. He's up there looking down at us, saying, I gave you exactly what you asked for. Why are you sad? Why are you stressed? Don't you know I already have this planned out for you?

When we don't accept the blessing the first time, we often find ourselves back in the same cycle, re-experiencing hardship or trauma in a different form. When we surrender our burdens, trust God's timing, and lean into His plan, we open ourselves up to joy, peace, and clarity, things we can never achieve by clinging to control.

SURRENDER IN THE CHAOS

Letting go doesn't mean giving up, it means giving *in* to the flow of life. Surrender is often misunderstood as weakness, but it's actually one of the most courageous decisions you can make. It doesn't mean you stop caring or stop trying; it means you stop fighting battles you were never meant to fight and stop gripping outcomes you were never meant to control.

Think about it like this:

If you're caught in a strong current, thrashing and resisting will only exhaust you. You'll tire yourself out long before you ever reach safety. When you loosen your grip and surrender, allowing yourself to float, the water can carry you to calmer shores.

Relinquishing control doesn't make the current less powerful, but it does conserve your strength for what comes next. It frees you from the panic of fighting what cannot be changed, and allows you to navigate life with steadier hands and a clearer mind.

TAKE ROOT

Releasing control is a process, not a one-time decision. It requires practice, patience, and a willingness to be honest about what is actually within your power. One of the most grounding lessons I learned came from a simple truth echoed in the Serenity Prayer: there are things we can change, things we cannot, and wisdom is required to know the difference.

Here's the formula I used to separate responsibility from control. It may help you, too.

1. The Serenity Statement

Take a few moments to write down the stressors currently weighing on you. As you list them, place each one into one of the two categories below.

Can Control:
- How I respond to challenges
- My daily habits and routines
- The boundaries I set
- The people I choose to surround myself with

Cannot Control:
- The past
- Other people's choices or reactions
- Outcomes I cannot predict
- Unexpected events

Once you've finished, read both lists slowly. Notice where your energy has been going. Are you exhausting yourself trying to control what was never yours to carry?

Keep this list somewhere visible. Let it serve as a daily reminder to release what is outside your control and to focus your strength, attention, and healing on what is within your reach.

2. The Release Journal

Once you've written your feelings, imagine releasing them into the hands of God.

- Write letters to your worries.
  For example: "Dear fear, I know you're trying to protect me, I need to let you go."

3. Reframe "What Ifs"

When you start spiraling into "what if" scenarios, reframe them with curiosity and possibility. For example:

- Instead of "What if everything goes wrong?"
  Try: "What if I'm stronger than I think I am?"

- Instead of "What if I can't handle this?"
  Try: "What if this is teaching me something valuable?"

4. Breath and Grounding

Practice grounding yourself in the present moment. Take a few deep breaths, place your hand over your heart, and remind yourself: "I am here. I am safe. I don't need all the answers right now."

SEED FOR THOUGHT

You don't have to figure everything out right now. You don't have to have all the answers. All you need to do is take the next step and let God meet you where you are.

**"The Lord will fight for you;
you need only to be still."**

Exodus 14:14

Four

BURIED STRENGTH

Resilience isn't something you're born with, it's something you build, moment by moment, decision by decision, through the fire and the quiet. Here's what I want you to remember: while resilience is cultivated, your capacity for it has been in you since the beginning. Spiritually, birth isn't just a physical event, it's the sacred entry point of your soul into this world, a divine appointment that signals the start of your unique journey. It's not random. It's not accidental. From the moment you took your first breath, there was intention written over your life. In many spiritual traditions, birth is seen as the crossing of a threshold, where your soul agrees to walk through this life with a purpose, a path, and an inner compass that will always try to guide you back to yourself and to God. Different cultures and beliefs may describe it differently, many agree on this: you came here with something already inside of you. A divine imprint. A knowing. A strength that was placed in you before you ever had to prove it.

As mentioned in the first chapter, from a Christian viewpoint, birth is not random, it's part of God's plan. Scripture teaches, *"Before I formed you in the womb, I knew you; before you were born, I set you apart..."* Jeremiah 1:5. You are not an accident; your life has meaning, even if you don't fully understand it yet.

Life is seen as a sacred gift from God. A time to grow spiritually, love, serve, and ultimately return to Him. The challenges and joys we face are part of a greater story, shaping us into who we are meant to be.

Birth symbolizes our entrance into a world of free will. While God has a plan, He also gives us the ability to make choices that shape our journey. Both light and darkness exist and our decisions influence how we grow, what we learn, and the impact we leave on others.

Some believe that our trials and challenges are not punishments, but opportunities, moments that refine us and bring us closer to God's purpose. The Bible teaches that each person is born with unique gifts and talents meant to serve others and glorify God: "We have different gifts, according to the grace given to each of us..." Romans 12:6.

Your birth was intentional, and so were the qualities placed inside you. The things that make you *you*, your personality, your talents, your passions are not accidents; they are tools meant to fulfill your calling and impact the world.

While birth is a divine beginning, life is about *becoming*. Spiritually, we grow through love, faith, and sometimes suffering. Many believe both joyful and difficult experiences are part of the process of becoming who we are meant to be.

The journey shapes us for something greater whether that's fulfilling a purpose here on Earth or preparing for eternity with God. No matter where you stand spiritually, one truth is clear: being born is more than

LEMON SEEDS

just entering the world; it's the start of something sacred. Your existence matters. Your life has meaning. Even when the journey feels hard, you were born for such a time as this.

Even if you don't yet fully understand your purpose, trust that it is there. As you walk through life—seeking, growing, and becoming—you will uncover the deeper meaning behind why you are here. Strength is not about never falling; it is about rising every single time you do. It's about taking just one more step when you feel you have nothing left. Even in your weakest moments, something inside you—be it God's grace, hope, or sheer purpose—will refuse to let you quit. This is the true definition of resilience.

Resilience isn't about avoiding pain or struggle; it's about choosing to move forward despite it. It's about trusting that, even in the toughest moments, God's hand is guiding you, shaping you, and preparing you for the greater purpose He has for your life.

From the outside, my life looked like it was progressing. I had overcome a lot and was achieving amazing milestones. I had a beautiful family, healthy kids, I was pursuing goals while becoming a version of myself I never thought possible. Inside that life, there was pain, unhealed trauma, and darkness I couldn't escape.

I relied heavily on my new-found faith. It was more than a belief it became my lifeline. I remember a quiet, weary moment when my then-husband looked at me, frustration thick in his voice, and asked, *"Why are we always tested in life? Why can't it just be easy?"* It was a fair question. One I had asked myself in silence many times. Without hesitation, I responded, *"I believe God is testing us to see if we are worthy of His next task in life, and He knows we are strong enough to endure the path He has for us."*

I hung onto the idea that our trials weren't punishments, but preparation. That the pain wasn't pointless, but purposeful. My optimism wasn't blind; it was a choice I made every single day to believe that if I had survived what I had survived, then there had to be something better ahead. Something meaningful. Something divine. Because if God was allowing me to walk through fire, then surely He was also planning to use it to refine me, not destroy me. That belief? That quiet, persistent faith? It carried me when nothing else could. I had to be completely honest there was a part of me that feared something terrible was right around the corner.

THE TEST

At one point, I felt completely stagnant in life. It was as if everything around me was moving, yet I was frozen in place. My marriage felt off like something deep beneath the surface was unraveling, even if I couldn't yet name it. There was a heaviness in my spirit that I couldn't shake. I found myself going through the motions, doing what I was supposed to do, saying what I was supposed to say internally, I was exhausted. Misaligned.

Then came one of the most honest moments of surrender I've ever experienced. I was standing in the shower water rushing over me, tears streaming down my face, and I felt this aching in my chest that I couldn't explain. With trembling lips and a heart wide open, I cried out to God not with fancy words, not with rehearsed faith, with raw desperation.

I said, *"God, if something in my life is holding me back, or isn't supposed to be part of my story, I give You full control. Remove it from me abruptly if You have to because then I'll know it's Your hand, not just chaos. God, I don't even know exactly what it is. I just know I feel stuck. I know You are guiding me, but right now it feels like we've stopped walking. So please, cleanse my life of what's not aligned with You. Strip away*

 LEMON SEEDS

what's no longer meant to stay. And guide me. Guide me boldly and clearly into the life You've destined for me."

That was the second most powerful prayer I've ever prayed.

At that moment, I wasn't asking for clarity, I was asking for cleansing. I wasn't begging for answers, I was surrendering my need to know and inviting God to take over completely. I wasn't seeking comfort, I was asking for divine disruption. Because deep down, I knew that real healing, real change, would come only when I stopped trying to control the outcome and let Him do what only He could.

That prayer? It changed everything.

Three months later, my life completely changed. A betrayal in my marriage was discovered that left me feeling hurt, discarded, and absolutely shattered. I remember the night I found out. I got into my car, and as soon as it turned on, the song *Look Up Child* by Lauren Daigle started playing. If you don't know the song, my favorite verse is the opening line: *"Where are You now when all I feel is doubt? Oh, where are You now when I can't figure it out? Oh, I, I-I-I, I hear You say, I hear You say, 'Look up, child.'"* In that moment, I knew that God was very present.

I want to be clear, I am not pro-divorce, nor do I believe that betrayal in a marriage automatically means divorce. We already experienced many trying times. There had been grace, understanding, and a lot of effort to keep God at the center of our marriage. Yet, we found ourselves here again. Very quickly after the discovery, our lives changed, and the only move for me was forward through the divorce process. To this day, it pains me to admit that this became the reality for us and for our kids. I would have done anything to save our marriage, sometimes God calls us to slay dragons. When He does, we better be ready to pick up the sword.

Once again, I found myself picking up the shattered pieces of my life, piece by piece. It wasn't a fun process. The person I spent all of my adulthood with had become a stranger. So much so that, a couple of years after we split, I was driving home and saw him on the side of the road from a very minor car accident. Instead of pulling over in a panic, I drove by feeling numb. I said a silent prayer for his safety, and, once I reached my destination, I sent him a quick message to make sure he was okay.

Isn't life strange in this sense? We go through moments that change how we handle situations and the people we hold dear. Moving forward from someone you love whether a parent, sibling, friend, or spouse is profoundly heartbreaking.

Life has a way of pushing us through things we once believed we couldn't survive. Here's the truth: It wasn't just the trials that defined me it was how I responded to them. I chose to keep walking. I chose to keep believing. I chose to keep trusting in God's plan, even when it felt impossible. I felt like an arrow being pulled all the way back, barely holding on, trusting that I would eventually be launched into the next part of my story.

There were moments during my divorce when I couldn't see a way through. I cried out to God, questioning why this was happening, and lay awake at night wondering how to rebuild my broken life. From past lessons, I knew healing doesn't come from avoiding hardship; it comes from walking through it, one step at a time, with grace and faith.

Divorce isn't easy and it's never a path someone chooses lightly. It feels like death in many ways, not just of a relationship, but of a shared future, of dreams built together, of an identity you carried for years. It's the unraveling of a life you once committed to, and no matter how broken it became, there's still grief attached to watching it fall apart. There's a deep mourning, not just for what was lost, but for what will never be.

 LEMON SEEDS

During my divorce, there were moments when it felt even harder than grieving the loss of my daughter. He was still in the same town, still exchanging the kids during visits, yet he had become someone I no longer recognized. In the middle of that heartbreak, I began to realize that God was doing something much deeper than just removing someone from my life. He was reaching into the depths of who I was and teaching me how to truly *let go*.

He was showing me that healing doesn't always come with closure tied up in a pretty bow. Sometimes it comes through surrender the kind where you stop waiting for the pain to disappear and start trusting Him in the middle of it. He was inviting me to release the grip I had on what I thought my life was supposed to look like and instead trust that what He had planned was better, even if I couldn't see it yet.

I remember a therapy session that completely shifted my mindset. I was venting, emotionally drained, expressing how everything felt broken, and how I needed to fix it. Fix my life, fix my kids' emotional well-being, fix the finances, fix the pain. I was taking on the weight of it all like it was my divine responsibility.

My therapist paused and said gently yet firmly, *"Nadine, you keep saying everything needs to be fixed. You talk about carrying all of this like it's your personal job to make everything whole again, for you and for everyone around you. So I have to ask you something. Do you see yourself as God?"*

I quickly responded. "Of course not, I know I'm not God."

She looked me in the eyes and said, *"Then stop trying to be. Let God be God."*

I sat there, stunned. Because at that moment, I realized how often I had been operating like the entire weight of the world rested on my shoulders. I wasn't just trying to hold my life together I was trying to control how it unfolded. I thought if I just worked harder, stayed stronger, gave more, *fixed* everything then it would all somehow make sense again.

In trying to fix everything, I was unintentionally pushing God's hand away. I was relying on my own strength, while praying for His intervention. I was exhausted not because I lacked faith, because I wasn't letting my faith carry me.

That conversation with my therapist was a holy interruption. A permission slip to stop striving and start surrendering. My job wasn't to hold everything together, it was to do the internal work of healing, of letting go, and of trusting that God could take what was shattered and make something sacred out of it.

That was the moment I stopped trying to be the savior of my story and allowed the real Savior to take His rightful place. It was in that surrender not in the fixing that I finally found peace.

I also realized I needed to get out of my emotions. I'd read this book called *The Breakup Bootcamp: The Science of Rewiring Your Heart* by Amy Chan, where she explains that emotions last for 90 seconds, it's the story we attach to them that makes them linger and shape our identity. I thought, *I could have moved past this in 90 seconds, yet here I am, a year later, still angry, resentful, and hurt.* That realization made me understand that I had to take responsibility for finding my God-given power again.

I returned to what had helped me in the past: journaling, therapy, and surrounding myself with supportive people. This time was different from when my daughter passed away. Instead of crying out in the air, I was intentionally crying out to God, asking Him to guide me through this part of my life.

I know now that healing isn't about a destination, it's about the journey.

     LEMON SEEDS

As painful as that journey was, I am grateful for it because it made me stronger and more resilient. The person I am today is not defined by my divorce or the betrayal I faced, it's defined by how I chose to respond to those experiences.

That said, I didn't always handle them in the most godly way. I had to learn to give myself grace because, despite my best intentions to rise above the pain, there were moments when my emotions got the best of me. The "90-second rule" went out the window, along with everyone involved in my pain, at least mentally.

When I think about my less than perfect moments, I remember a message I heard at a Brandon Lake concert. In between sets, he shared a powerful testimony. Although he was speaking to the entire crowd, it felt like he was speaking directly to me. I won't quote him word for word, the essence of his message was this: Yes, we strive to live a Christ-like life, but we are not Jesus. We will sin and need forgiveness, that's why Jesus died on the cross. So, do your best to be the best version of yourself, give yourself grace and forgiveness when you fall short. Because of Jesus, you are already forgiven.

His message reached the depths of my soul. I felt an incredible weight lift from my shoulders, a relief from the burdens I had been carrying, of all the moments I didn't show up at my best.

Many times I asked God, "Why? Why is this happening? What am I supposed to do now?" I felt His presence, quiet yet strong, reminding me that I wasn't alone. He whispered to my heart: *You are not finished. This is not the end of your story.*

To my realization and relief, my story was still being written. The pages didn't stop turning just because my heart was broken or my plans had fallen apart. I had spent so long thinking that the worst moments of my life were the end of the story, the final punctuation mark on dreams I once held dear. They weren't. They were merely commas. Pauses. Plot twists. Necessary tension in the middle of a narrative that still had more to say.

I began to understand that the things I thought disqualified me were actually the very things God would use to define the next chapter. That realization changed everything. My failures didn't erase my future. My grief didn't disqualify me from joy. My setbacks weren't signs that I was off course. They were evidence that I was being rerouted toward something deeper. Something fuller. Something eternal.

There was still breath in my lungs. Still stirring in my spirit. Still dreams I hadn't yet dreamed and places I hadn't yet walked into. There was still *hope*, not the flimsy kind that depends on good days and perfect outcomes, the kind that roots itself in the promises of God. There was still *purpose*, not just in spite of what I'd walked through, but because of it.

Once I saw that, I started to live like it. In the times I couldn't let go of the racing thoughts, the endless attempts to connect the dots on what led to this moment, and the blame I heaped on myself. I convinced myself I hadn't been a good wife, if I had just cooked that dinner when I was exhausted or folded that pile of laundry instead of focusing on my business, my family would still be together. The truth is, there are situations where you could move the stars in the sky, and it still wouldn't be good enough for the people who aren't meant to embrace the beauty of what you offer.

As I began to heal this part of me, I also began to rediscover myself. I realized that I had spent so much of my life living for others, trying to be everything to everyone, that I had lost sight of who I truly was. Honestly, having been in a relationship since I was 18 and a mother by 19, I had no idea who Nadine was outside the titles. Now, I had the chance to recon-

     LEMON SEEDS

nect with myself and find joy in simple things, and build a new life on God's terms.

It wasn't easy, and it wasn't immediate. Healing takes time, and growth isn't linear. Some days I felt like I was making progress, and other days, I felt like I had taken ten steps back. Even then, I was advancing. Through it all, I kept reminding myself that I didn't need to have everything figured out all at once. All I needed was to keep moving forward.

RETURNING TO WHO YOU WERE CREATED TO BE

After experiencing a traumatic loss, returning to your past self becomes nearly impossible, as that version of you may start to feel unsafe during the healing process. You might question how you allowed yourself to be in certain situations, how could you be blind? Stupid? This is where a lot of people start to build a wall to block anyone ever getting close to them again, when you do this you block out so many beautiful parts of life that are waiting for you.

Trauma changes us, sometimes in painful or unfair ways. However, those changes can lead to new beginnings. No matter how much we hurt, God is always working to redeem our stories. He doesn't waste any pain. Every challenge, every heartbreak, shapes us into the people we are meant to be.

Your pain is producing something, it's working, shaping, preparing, refining… even when you can't see it.

2 Corinthians 4:17 shows this to be true, "For our light and momentary troubles are achieving for us an eternal glory that far outweighs them all."

Now, when I look back on that season, I see those events differently. What once felt like brokenness became a place of growth. What once felt like an ending revealed itself as the beginning of something new. I don't romanticize the struggle or minimize its cost, but I honor what it taught me.

I don't regret the lessons I learned or the strength that was built in me along the way. While I would never choose the pain that brought me here, I no longer reject the person I became because of it. I learned how to stand whole—not because everything was repaired, but because I stopped abandoning myself in the process.

There are still days when the pain of my divorce and loss resurfaces. I no longer fight it or rush to push it away. Instead, I let it exist without allowing it to define me. I hold space for both joy and sorrow, knowing they are not opposites, but companions in the human experience. Through it all, I've discovered that I am capable of far more than I ever believed.

If you are walking through a season of heartache, loss, or unexpected change, hear this clearly: what you are experiencing is real, and it matters. I know that may feel hard to believe, because grief has a way of isolating us—convincing us that no one could possibly understand the depth of our pain.

Even in the moments when you feel most unseen, you are not forgotten. God is nearer than you feel, closer than your grief allows you to recognize. While others may not see the silent battles you fight or understand the weight you carry, your struggle is not invisible—and neither are you.

TAKE ROOT

Leading Your Emotions

Strong emotions are not a sign of weakness, they are information. After seasons of loss or divorce, emotions can rise quickly and feel overwhelming. This exercise is about learning how to respond to what you feel without letting it control you.

 LEMON SEEDS

1. Name the emotion before reacting.

When a strong emotion shows up, pause and write it down. Don't explain it. Just name it: anger, sadness, fear, resentment, relief, confusion. Naming the emotion creates space between feeling and reaction.

2. Locate it in your body.

Ask yourself: *Where do I feel this?*
Tight chest. Heavy shoulders. Shallow breath. Awareness helps calm the nervous system.

3. Choose your response.

Write one sentence that begins with:
Even though I feel ___, I choose to ___.
(Example: Even though I feel angry, I choose to pause before responding.)

4. Release what isn't yours to carry.

Write down what this emotion is tempting you to control—another person, an outcome, a conversation. Acknowledge it, then release it.

5. Ground yourself in the present moment.

Take three slow breaths. On each exhale, remind yourself:
I can feel this without being ruled by it.

SEED FOR THOUGHT

Your struggle today is the testimony you'll stand on tomorrow.

You already have everything you need in this moment, and the very breath in your lungs is proof that God is not finished with you.

"And we know that in all things God works
for the good of those who love Him."

Romans 8:28

Five

IT'S ALL GRIEF

When I used to hear the word *grief*, I would immediately associate it with death or the loss of someone I loved, what I've come to learn is that grief shows up in so many more places, It manifests in many forms through heartbreak, betrayal, unfulfilled dreams, and even the loss of who we once were. While the stages of grief are linked to death, they apply to any significant loss. The emotional upheaval of grief can feel overwhelming, it's crucial to understand that it's a natural and necessary part of healing. Even the most painful experiences can foster resilience and a deeper understanding of who we truly are.

I've encountered grief in many areas of my life. When my daughter passed away, when I had to let go of the life I envisioned for myself, through the end of friendships, during my business journey, and through divorce. I'm convinced there are more, mundane daily things that eventually we grieve over. I didn't realize I was grieving anything other than my daughter's death until I recognized that any significant change in life forces us to pick up the pieces and navigate new terrain, leaving us feeling uneasy, uncertain, and often fearful.

Healing is a process, and by acknowledging each phase, we can move forward on our journey. While the emotions of what once was may not vanish completely, we'll eventually stand strong, able to declare that grief no longer has a hold on us.

Once I understood grief and how it shows up, I was able to confront it head-on and take control of where it led me. Without that understanding how to handle grief, grief will handle you. You, my friend, are on the path to not just surviving, but owning what survival looks like for you. I don't want you to think of survival as simply getting up, breathing, and saying "I made it through the day." There will be days when that's all you can give, and those days are victories, too. Know this: as a beautiful child of God, you were meant to thrive. Each day is a gift, especially after surviving something you thought would bury you.

You won't be stuck faking smiles or robotically replying "I'm fine" when asked how you are. You will be more than fine. If you allow it, you can be filled with joy and wholeness, even when it feels like a part of you is missing. If you're ready for that, let's dive into the next few pages with the intention to face the emotions that no longer need to control you. Buckle up, because we're about to take back your power!

STAGE 1: THIS CAN'T BE HAPPENING
DENIAL

When you experience a loss, one of the first thoughts that rushes through your mind is, *"This can't be happening."*

After the initial impact of the car accident that claimed the life of my daughter, my eyes opened to shattered glass embedded in my hands. I looked over at my partner, his body limp like a pile of laundry. Then I turned to Jaylin, she was suddenly asleep. My mind refused to accept what my eyes were seeing. *This can't be happening.*

 LEMON SEEDS

From the agonizing decision to take her off life support to coming home to a house that was far too quiet, to planning her funeral, I kept thinking over and over, *This can't be real.* Even though I was physically present for all of it, I couldn't accept that this was my reality.

For years, I talked endlessly about Jaylin as if she were still alive. I told myself I was keeping her memory alive, the truth was, I couldn't admit she was gone. Every time I had to say it out loud, I immediately followed it up with how she was still present in our lives. I was in denial because I couldn't bear the thought that she was no longer part of me today, tomorrow, or the next day.

Denial is the mind's way of protecting itself from the shock of loss. I clung to the comfort of my memories because facing the truth was too painful. Speaking of her life in the present tense reassured me that she was still here, so I didn't have to fully acknowledge the devastating reality.

How Denial Shows Up

- You may convince yourself that everything will get better or it's just a phase.

- You may refuse to acknowledge the pain, pushing it down instead of facing it.

- You may speak about someone or something in the present tense as a way of holding on.

Take Root

Take a moment to acknowledge the reality of your situation. Allow yourself to sit with the discomfort instead of pushing it away. Journaling or talking to someone you trust can help you process what's happening. Give yourself permission to mourn and fully feel the weight of your emotions. This doesn't make you weak, it makes you human.

STAGE 2: WHY DID THIS HAPPEN TO ME? ANGER

When you begin to grasp the weight of your reality, anger can feel like an unstoppable force. It surges through your veins, giving you a sense of power when you're most vulnerable. You may become guarded, quick to react, and carry an energy that warns others, *Don't even look at me.*

At first, anger can feel productive, it fuels you, shielding you from helplessness. Over time, it becomes a heavy burden, one we were never meant to carry long-term.

I remember the day I threw the vase across my house, watching it shatter against the wall. For a brief moment, it felt good. I was furious at what my life had become. I had been a good mother why did God think I deserved this? The broken shards mirrored how I felt inside.

During my divorce, anger was my constant companion, from sunrise to sunset. I felt discarded after pouring 15 years into a relationship. The lack of communication between us made it even worse. I never got the closure I needed. His excuse boiled down to *"You're not the 18-year-old I fell in love with, and I don't want to meal prep on Mondays,"* I was enraged. That's all I got after 15 years? It made no sense and felt deeply unfair. Anger was easier than trying to understand it.

Maybe you've been there too, when someone's actions or words felt completely unjustified, and your anger became a shield. It made you feel strong, like you were taking back control. Here's the truth: sitting in anger blocks the good that is meant to come from the situation. It stops the light that's supposed to break through.

Anger is heavy. The longer you carry it, the more it weighs you down. When you release it, you're free to move forward.

LEMON SEEDS

How Anger Shows Up

- Resentment toward the person who hurt you

- Guardedness, making it hard to trust others

- Frustration and a loss of joy in things that once fulfilled you

Take Root

Allow yourself to feel enraged, but don't let it control you. Find healthy ways to release it through physical activity, creative expression, or talking to a trusted friend or professional. Use your outrage as fuel to push forward, not as an anchor that keeps you stuck in bitterness.

STAGE 3: MAYBE IF I DO THIS… BARGAINING

Bargaining is the stage where we search desperately for ways to undo the pain, making silent deals with ourselves, others, or even God. *Maybe if I had done this differently, things would have turned out another way.* It's the mind's attempt to regain control in a situation where we feel completely powerless.

Of all the stages of grief, bargaining can be one of the most damaging. It traps us in a cycle of self-blame, convincing us that a different choice could have changed everything. We rewrite history in our minds, questioning every decision and falsely believing we somehow deserved what happened because we *must* have missed a step along the way.

I remember the night of the accident vividly. As I exited my apartment complex, I hesitated over which route to take. I asked my partner, and he said, *"Whatever way you feel most safe."* After the crash, that moment played on repeat in my mind. *What if I had taken the other route? Would she still be here?* That single *what if* haunted me and nearly broke me.

Here's what I've learned: Some events unfold simply because they were meant to. You couldn't have avoided them. You couldn't have done better. You made the best possible choice with the information you had. You did not fail. You did not deserve what happened.

Give yourself permission to release the burden of thinking you could have controlled the uncontrollable.

How Bargaining Shows Up

- Obsessing over what you could have done differently.

- Regretting not seeing the warning signs sooner.

- Replaying past events, searching for a different outcome.

Take Root

Let go of the *what-ifs* and *if-onlys*. Understand that your circumstances are not your fault. Healing does not come from rewriting the past, it comes from deciding how you'll move forward. When you catch yourself bargaining, remind yourself: *I made the best decision I could at that time. That is enough.*

STAGE 4: I DON'T KNOW HOW I CAN GO ON DEPRESSION

Depression sets in when the weight of loss becomes undeniable. It brings deep sadness, loneliness, and sometimes hopelessness. At first, support surrounds you, friends check in, family makes sure you have food and other necessities. Eventually, the dust settles. Life moves forward for everyone else, but for you, time seems frozen at the moment of your loss.

You may find yourself trapped in a cycle, one moment smiling at beautiful memories, and the next seething with fury that they were stolen from you. If left unchecked, that emotional pendulum slows, and suddenly,

 LEMON SEEDS

leaving you numb. Sadness, once an unwelcome visitor, becomes a constant companion. Isolation feels easier than facing the world.

If you're anything like I was, you learned to wear the mask well. Standing in a room full of people, smiling and laughing, while inside you're wrecked. At night, the weight of your reality crashes down, stealing whatever joy you managed to find that day. Survival becomes your goal: just get through the day without breaking down. Looking in the mirror, you barely recognize the person behind the forced smile, the most broken version of yourself.

I learned that isolation and depression are fertile ground for darkness. Being alone in my pain only made it heavier. I needed people who wouldn't just pity me but would pour life back into me. Spaces where I could speak my pain out loud, name it, and release it.

Maybe you don't have family or friends who truly understand, however I promise there are people who *want* to help—support groups, online communities, counselors. Lifelines are everywhere if you're willing to reach for them.

If this is your current stage, I have one plea: Don't stay in the darkness too long. I know it feels like this pain will last forever, it won't. Even if you can't see it yet, the sun will rise again. Joy will come in the morning. Hold on a little longer, and whatever you do, don't stop fighting for your healing.

How Depression Shows Up

- Emotional overwhelm, loneliness, and emptiness. A loss of joy or meaning.

- Hopelessness, wondering if wholeness is possible.

Take Root

Allow yourself to grieve, don't allow isolation to consume you. Seek professional help, connect with someone who genuinely cares, or engage in activities that nourish your soul. Healing takes time, and it's okay to feel sadness. Sadness is a season, not a destination. Keep moving forward, even if it's one small step at a time.

STAGE 5: I AM READY TO MOVE FORWARD ACCEPTANCE

Acceptance is when we come to terms with loss and choose to move forward. It's not about forgetting, it's about finding peace and embracing life again.

For me, acceptance looked different depending on the loss. It took 14 years to come to terms with my daughter's passing, but only two years for my divorce. The difference wasn't just time, it was my willingness to seek understanding. I resisted God for years, blaming Him for my suffering. I couldn't comprehend how He allowed such pain. When I opened my heart to a bigger picture beyond loss, I started understanding how God works.

My spiritual mama, Jeannine, shifted my perspective when she shared a famous quote from Albert Einstein: "You are either living as if everything is a miracle, or as if nothing is a miracle." My mind instantly raced through all the hard times I had endured, and with each heartbreaking moment, I could trace it to a miracle that followed, as if I would never have experienced one without the other.

Even my divorce, as painful as it was, had divine purpose. When I stopped resisting, I saw how every piece of my journey shaped me into who I am today. My pain gave me the ability to reach others in their darkest moments and offer hope. That was God's gift to me turning what was meant to break me into something that brought light to others.

When life hands you lemons, don't just make lemonade. Recognizing the lemons are a gift. Accept them, and use them to create something sweeter, richer, and more meaningful.

How Acceptance Shows Up

- Finding peace with what happened without needing to approve of it.

- Forgiving, not for others, but for your healing and freedom.

- Shifting focus from what you've lost to what you can still create.

Take Root

Embrace your new reality and take small steps to rebuild. Set goals, create routines, and focus on growth. Your story isn't over,this is a new beginning. Let it be beautiful.

SEED FOR THOUGHT

Grief is messy and unpredictable, but it's part of a process. It's universal, and you are entitled to every emotion that comes with it. Healing is an ebb and flow dance. Some days you'll move forward, and other days you'll feel stuck. Every step counts as progress.

Jesus Himself promises comfort *in* grief, not after it.

**"Blessed are those who mourn,
for they will be comforted."**

Matthew 5:4

~ Six ~

WATERING THE DRY PLACES

Life has a way of knocking us down. Just when you think you've caught your breath, another wave hits. Loss, disappointment, and heartbreak can weigh so heavily that standing back up feels impossible.

Here's what I've learned: staying down isn't an option.

There comes a moment when you have to decide:

Will I stay buried under the dirt of what happened, or will I choose to rise?

Standing back up doesn't mean pretending the pain never existed. It doesn't mean acting unbothered or unaffected. It means refusing to let the pain define you, shape you, or silence you.

It's that quiet moment deep inside where you finally realize:
Even though I didn't choose what happened to me… I *can* choose what happens next.

It's the beginning of reclaiming yourself. It's the moment you go from surviving to rebuilding. It's the moment the dry places in your life begin to thirst for something new.

FACING THE FALL

Think back to the first time you felt pain. Maybe it was a scraped knee from falling off your bike. Maybe it was betrayal by a friend. Maybe it was losing a pet or feeling unloved by someone who should've protected you.

For me, it was when I was about four or five years old. I had just woken up from a nap and wandered into the bathroom. Back then, toilet décor was a thing, imagine your shaggy bathroom rug, wrapped around the toilet seat. Hideous *and* hazardous.

Half-asleep, I reached to flush the toilet, and missed the handle thanks to that thick cover. At the same time, I slipped on the matching rug.

My face hit the rim of the toilet bowl. Hard. My two front teeth? Gone. There was blood everywhere. I remember my mom running in, panicked. The ride to the hospital. The stitches in my lip. The confusion. The pain.

That was my first taste of physical trauma. At such a young age, I didn't dwell on the pain it caused. I didn't grow up afraid of the toilet. I didn't swear off flushing or decide bathrooms were dangerous places. The fall happened. The injury healed. I told my mom to take off that ridiculous cover, and life moved on.

I didn't run. I didn't hide. I didn't pretend I wasn't scared.

Still, here I am, 36 years old, and sometimes, if my foot slips even a little, that same surge of fear shoots through my body. A visceral flashback.

LEMON SEEDS

We often think trauma lives only in our memories, but it lives in our bodies too. Even when our minds try to forget, our bodies remember. They carry tension, fear, and grief quietly, sometimes for years. You may not realize how much your body is holding until it begins to speak through pain, fatigue, illness, or anxiety. That isn't weakness. It's your nervous system trying to protect you.

Your nervous system does exactly what it was designed to do: protect you. When threatened, it shifts into fight, flight, freeze, or fawn to help you survive. The challenge is that when trauma goes unprocessed, the body never receives the signal that the danger has passed. Instead, it remains stuck in survival mode. You may feel constantly on edge, emotionally numb, or deeply exhausted without fully understanding why. That isn't just in your head. It's your body remembering.

You may experience:

Tension in the muscles. Think about the last time you were scared, your shoulders tightened, your jaw clenched, your stomach knotted. Imagine living with that tension daily. Unresolved trauma causes the body to brace, to literally tighten up as a shield. Over time, that protective response becomes chronic. It can lead to headaches, back pain, joint issues, or even autoimmune flare-ups. The body holds what the heart hasn't had space to heal.

Fascia holds the memories. Your fascia, the thin layer of connective tissue that wraps around your muscles, organs, and nerves, is like the emotional archive of your body. It stores everything: experiences, stress, and suppressed emotions.

That's why certain stretches, yoga poses, or massages can bring up unexpected tears or waves of emotion. You're not losing it, you're releasing what's been buried.

Breath becomes shallow. Trauma disrupts the breath.
You might catch yourself holding it, breathing fast, or staying in a shallow chest pattern. This is the body's way of minimizing sensation and staying in alert mode. Long-term, it keeps your system locked in stress. Deep, slow breaths tell your body: You're safe now.
That's where healing begins.

The gut stores emotional pain. The gut is often called your "second brain" for a reason. It's wired to your emotions through the vagus nerve. When trauma or prolonged stress hits, your digestion suffers bloating, nausea, IBS, or appetite loss aren't random. They're signs your body is processing something deeper. Because grief, fear, and emotional pain don't just live in your heart, they live in your gut, too.

The body triggers flashbacks. Have you ever smelled something and suddenly felt anxious, even though nothing was wrong? Or heard a sound that made your heart race without warning? That's a somatic memory-when the body reacts before the mind understands why. Because trauma is often stored as sensation, not logic.

When your body senses something familiar, it responds like it's happening again even if it's not. This is why healing isn't just about thinking your way through it. It's about feeling your way through it. Your body is part of your healing not a barrier to it.

I was so over feeling the side effects of things I had faced in life that I decided to take a Mental Health Wellness Coach course, I ended with a Certificate of Completion, but the true reward was understanding what my body was facing. For so many years of just trying to get through the pain, I felt sick inside. I thought there was a severe diagnosis that my blood work was going to reveal, truthfully it was the pain of all the stuff I was holding on to unknowingly.

LEMON SEEDS

GOD MADE YOUR BODY TO REMEMBER AND HEAL

What science now explains, Scripture revealed long ago:
your body is not separate from your spirit. God created you as a whole being. What affects your heart affects your flesh, and what weighs on your spirit shows up in your body.

The Bible says,

"A cheerful heart is good medicine, but a crushed spirit dries up the bones." — Proverbs 17:22

Long before trauma research existed, God already told us that emotional pain impacts our physical health. A crushed spirit, unhealed grief, or held-in sorrow can literally "dry the bones" a poetic but accurate description of how trauma drains the strength from the body. The Bible is full of testimonies that confirm this.

David, who knew deep anguish, cried out:

**"My heart pounds, my strength fails
me... my body has no health because of
my sin and grief." Psalm 38:8,10**

He wasn't just emotionally overwhelmed, his physical body felt the weight of his distress.

This is what trauma does. This is what unprocessed pain does. It embeds itself in the body until healing is allowed to begin.

Here is the hope:
Just as the body remembers the pain, it also remembers *how to heal*. God designed your nervous system, your breath, your heart, and even your tears as part of your healing process. Nothing about the way your body reacts is a flaw. It's a divine design.

God meets you in the very places trauma has touched. He doesn't ask you to pretend. He doesn't ask you to "get over it." He draws near to your brokenness, your tight chest, trembling hands, racing thoughts, and aching gut and reminds you:

You don't have to stay stuck in survival mode.
Your body is allowed to let go.
You are called to be restored.

The same God who knit your body together is the One who restores it. Every breath you release, every tear you shed, every tension that softens, is evidence of His work in you.

TAKE ROOT

I want you to take a moment and check in with your body.
Not your mind, your body.

Which of these have *you* felt?

- Have you ever lived in survival mode, always waiting for the next hit to come?

- Do you carry tension in your neck, shoulders, or jaw that never quite seems to go away?

- Have you ever cried during a stretch or massage and didn't know why?

- Do you find yourself holding your breath without realizing it?

- Have stomach issues or appetite changes followed seasons of emotional pain?

- Have you ever felt a physical reaction: tight chest, racing heart, knot in your stomach without knowing what triggered it?

These aren't random. They're your body waving a flag, saying: *There's still something here.* It's okay.

You're not broken. You're holding more than you were ever meant to carry alone.

CHOOSING TO HEAL

With all the conversations happening around mental health today, it's easy to think healing is as simple as going to therapy.
"Just talk to someone, and you'll feel better," right?

Listen. I'm a huge advocate for therapy. I even became a certified mental wellness coach because I believe in it so much. Healing goes deeper than just talking about it.

When my daughter passed away, I talked about her every chance I got. It comforted me. It reminded me she was real. That I got to be her mother. That our one year together was sacred and not a dream.

When I was walking through the pain of divorce, I talked about it too. How angry I was. How discarded I felt. How much it broke me. Talking about it helped me feel seen. It validated what I was going through.

Here's what I had to learn:
Talking about it alone wasn't enough.

I had to face the deep roots of my pain. I had to sit with it. Feel it. Understand it. Eventually, I had to make a choice:
To stop rehearsing the pain and start reclaiming my healing.

That choice didn't happen overnight. It wasn't one big moment. It was a million small ones.

It's a process I want to walk you through because I know what it feels like to be stuck. To feel like you're drowning in grief, spinning in heartbreak, unsure if you'll ever come up for air again.

I want to remind you, you will.

You're going to get every last drop of what helped me rise, every lesson, every truth, every tool I found on my way back to life. Because just like that moment when I stood back up after my first childhood fall, you are meant to get back up too.

No matter what life has thrown at you. No matter how deep the ache. You are not meant to stay down.

THE SECRET SAUCE TO STANDING BACK UP

Choosing to stand back up isn't about time passing or hoping things magically get better. It's an intentional decision to reclaim your power, even when everything in you feels broken. It's about rewiring your mind, healing your body, and rebuilding your life from the inside out.

This is the *exact process* I used when life tried to bury me.

1. Feel It Fully (Don't Rush the Process)

We live in a world that tells us to "move on" quickly. Grief makes people uncomfortable. Sadness is inconvenient. Pain that doesn't come with a tidy bow gets dismissed. True healing begins when you let yourself *feel* without shame or a deadline.

I'll never forget the day I was venting to a family member about my ex-husband, and they cut me off with, *"Just get over it already."*

That sentence lit a fire in me. I hung up the phone, sat there in disbelief, and had an entire conversation with myself:

   LEMON SEEDS

How dare they? I'm angry. I'm hurt. I'm walking through things no one else has seen, and I'm just supposed to get over it?

No. Not this time.

I realized I wasn't wrong for feeling. I was finally releasing the truth and putting a name to it. I don't have to get over it. Instead, I'll deal with it before it takes over me.

This is how I was raised: sweep it under the rug, don't cry over spilled milk, keep it moving. So much of my life was built on suppressing emotion and pretending everything was fine. That's where the image of "Nadine, you're so strong" came from.

The truth? I wasn't strong. I was just a professional at *faking it.*

When my daughter passed away, by the time the funeral came, I had pulled myself together enough to smile and thank people for coming, while dying inside. That wasn't strength. That was survival.

During my divorce, my kids witnessed some of my lowest moments. We were living in one room at my parents' house, no privacy, no peace. I cried in the car before school pickup. In the shower before bed.

My kids would ask, *"Mom, have you been crying?"* and I'd lie through tears: *"No, I'm fine."*

Then one day, my therapist asked me, *"Who told you you can't cry in front of your children?"*

Like every time my therapist asked me a self reflecting question, I froze. "No one," I answered. "But… what am I teaching them if I do?"

She looked me in the eyes and said, *"You're teaching them it's okay to feel. You're giving them permission to be human. That's how you break generational curses."*

That moment changed everything for me.

By allowing myself to *feel*, I gave my kids a safe space to feel too.

Let yourself cry. Scream. Write. Talk. Be silent. Stop trying to be "strong" by pretending you're fine. Strength is found in allowing yourself to be human.

What I did:

I stopped numbing with busyness.

I cried when I needed to.

I wrote letters to people who hurt me even if I never sent them.

I let the grief move through me instead of trying to outrun it.

2. Recognize That Pain Is a Teacher

Pain is uncomfortable, yes. It's also one of the greatest teachers you'll ever have. It reveals what needs attention. It exposes patterns. It stretches you toward growth.

Instead of asking, *"Why did this happen to me?"* try asking:

- What is this trying to teach me?

- What pattern am I repeating?

- What do I need to release to stop coming back here?

What I did:

I stopped seeing pain as punishment.

I started seeing it as an invitation to rise, to grow, to become.

 LEMON SEEDS

3. Take Your Power Back (Rewrite the Narrative)

Trauma can steal your voice, your trust, your confidence. Healing begins when you change the story you tell yourself.

Yes, terrible things happened. They don't get to define you.

Shift your self-talk:

- From *"I'll never recover"* to *"I'm healing every day."*

- From *"I'll never feel whole again"* to *"I'm creating a new version of wholeness."*

What I did:

I stopped saying "I'll never trust again."
Instead, I said, "I'm learning to trust myself again."

4. Get It Out of Your Body

Trauma lives in the body. If you don't release it, it festers turning into anxiety, chronic pain, or emotional numbness.

You have to move it out. Move your body. Stretch. Walk. Dance. Shake. Breathe deep. Do the work physically, not just mentally.

What I did:

I started moving my body every day.
I practiced breathing.

5. Reconnect with Your Faith and Purpose

When you're in pain, it's easy to feel disconnected from Jesus, from your identity, from your purpose. Your pain is not wasted. Talk to Jesus. Even if you're angry. Even if you're confused. He can take it.

Ask yourself:

- What am I meant to learn from this?

- How can I use this pain to help others?

- What purpose is being born through this suffering?

What I did:

I prayed even when I didn't feel like it.
I vented to Jesus when I needed to.
I reminded myself: *He's not afraid of my pain.*
I started to turn my pain into purpose. That's what brought me back to life.

6. Choose to Rise (Again and Again)

There will be days you feel like you're thriving, and days you feel like you're barely breathing.

That's okay. What matters is that you keep choosing to rise.

Even if it's messy.
Even if it's slow.
Even if it's just one small step at a time.

What I did:

I gave myself grace.

LEMON SEEDS

I stopped waiting for a "magically healed" version of myself. Instead, I showed up daily with what I had, how I was, and where I was.

THIS IS YOUR MOMENT

I want you to hear me:

You are stronger than you think. You have what it takes to stand back up. This isn't just about survival. This is about rebirth. This is about choosing life again.

And again.

And again.

On the other side of this pain is a version of you that's wiser, softer, and more powerful than you've ever known. Let's take that first step together.

SEED FOR THOUGHT

If no one has told you this lately *you're doing better than you think.* You are not behind. You are not broken. You are in process. There is still *so much beauty ahead.* Trust that your becoming is a process He's committed to seeing through.

"Being confident of this, that He who began a good work in you will carry it on to completion until the day of Christ Jesus."

Philippians 1:6

Seven

FINDING YOUR ROOTS

When life falls apart, it doesn't just hurt, it disorients you. Suddenly, nothing feels stable. The people you once trusted don't feel safe anymore. The identity you built no longer fits. Even your sense of self feels unfamiliar, like you're standing in a place you don't recognize.

That's what trauma does. It doesn't just break your heart, it fractures your sense of where you are and who you are.

You begin drifting emotionally, mentally, spiritually. One moment you feel fine, and the next you're consumed by a memory, a trigger, or a wave of emotion that seems to come out of nowhere. You start questioning yourself, your reactions, even your sanity.

There were many moments I found myself self-diagnosing with every mental health disorder under the sun not because I was searching for a label, but because I didn't recognize myself anymore. I felt disconnected from who I used to be, disoriented by grief, pain, and uncertainty. I wasn't looking for answers as much as I was looking for a way to come back to myself when everything felt unsteady.

Over time, I learned that real growth doesn't happen at the surface. It begins beneath it.

A lemon tree doesn't grow by forcing fruit first. It grows by strengthening what can't be seen. Long before anything blooms, its roots spread deep into the soil searching for water, anchoring for stability, drawing nourishment from places untouched by sun or wind. The deeper the roots grow, the more resilient the tree becomes. It doesn't rush this process. It can't. Without healthy roots, no amount of sunlight or effort can produce lasting fruit.

In the same way, God often does His deepest work in the places no one else can see, not even us. While we're focused on what's visible, what's broken, or what feels delayed, He's strengthening what will sustain us long-term. He tends to the roots quietly, patiently, without rushing the process. Even when we feel stagnant or unsure, God is still at work beneath the surface building stability, restoring trust, and preparing us to carry what's coming next.

That's why finding your roots matters.

Because if you're going to keep moving forward, you need something beneath the surface, something that sustains you when life shifts again. Growth doesn't come from reacting to every change around you. It comes from staying connected to what nourishes you from within.

I wish I could tell you I understood this early on, that I was grounded from the beginning. The truth is, I wasn't.

Before my marriage ended, I thought the things keeping me steady were external. Social media. Venting. Validation. I poured my heart out online, convinced that if I shared enough, I'd feel better. When I look back at

　　　LEMON SEEDS

some of those posts from years ago, I don't cringe because I was honest, I cringe because I was desperate for someone else to carry what I didn't yet know how to hold myself.

I leaned heavily on friends and family, not just for support, but for confirmation. I wanted reassurance that what I went through really was painful, really was unfair, hoping that if enough people agreed with me, it would somehow make the pain easier to carry.

It helped… briefly.

But I always ended up in the same place empty, exhausted, and still untethered.

I joined support groups. I went to therapy. I poured myself into helping others, thinking that if I could guide someone else through their pain, then maybe mine wouldn't be for nothing. No matter how productive or helpful it looked on the outside, internally I still felt like I was floating through life without a foundation.

When my marriage ended and I found myself truly alone, something shifted.

That was when I stopped negotiating my faith and fully surrendered. I allowed God to become my foundation, not a backup plan, not a last resort, not a spiritual add-on. The One I leaned on completely.

For the first time in my life, I wasn't praying to check a box. I was praying because I didn't know how to get through the next moment. I wasn't reading Scripture to feel "spiritual." I was reading it to survive and to remember that if God had healed and restored others, He could meet me too.

Did that mean I suddenly handled everything perfectly?

Absolutely not.

I'm human, just like you. I still had emotions, reactions, setbacks. What this gave me instead was space. Space to pause. Space to reflect. Space to ask better questions.

Who am I becoming now?

What kind of life do I want to build from here?

I think a lot of people misunderstand what it means to have a relationship with God. I'm not religious, and I've always said that my relationship with Him is personal and honest. I hope yours is too.

When I say God became my foundation, I mean He met me in my rawest pain. I could bring Him the same questions, the same frustrations, the same fears—over and over again—and He never told me to "get over it." He didn't shame me. He didn't rush me.

He loved me. He challenged me. He invited me to grow. To find my voice. To create boundaries. To step into courage, confidence, and purpose. To release the shame, guilt, anxiety, and depression that had taken root in my body.

To do that, I had to walk through every hard part. I had to feel every feeling. I had to allow myself to be formed into who I am today.

There's a moment that still stands out to me.

Sitting in church with my kids, just like we do most Sundays. During worship—hands raised, tears falling—they'd look up at me and ask, *"Mom, are you okay?"* And in that moment, I realized something I hadn't fully named yet: that space, that release, was where I felt safest. It wasn't performance. It wasn't strength. It was permission.

　　　　LEMON SEEDS

In worship, I let it all go. I stopped holding everything together. I laid down the weight I'd been carrying all week. It became my weekly surrender—and I cherished it deeply.

But over time, surrender didn't stay contained to a building or a single hour.

It followed me home. It met me in my room late at night when my thoughts wouldn't slow down. It showed up in my car, gripping the steering wheel, whispering prayers through tears at red lights. It found me in the shower, water running, finally exhaling after a long day. Surrender became less about where I was and more about how I lived.

I learned that I didn't need music playing or hands raised to lay things down. I could do it in the quiet, in the chaos, in the middle of ordinary moments. Piece by piece, I stopped carrying everything alone.

And that's the reminder I still return to, again and again:

I don't have to carry it all by myself.

THE BACKPACK EXERCISE

I want to share something with you that's helped me stay grounded in moments of emotional overwhelm.

It's something I now call the *Backpack to Jesus* moment.

When you're going through something heavy, and you feel yourself wanting to react or spiral, pause. Close your eyes. Picture yourself holding a backpack.

Now, one by one, begin to name every emotion you're feeling and *stuff it in there:*

"Anxiety- you're going in."

"Anger- you too."

"Frustration- yep, there's still room."

"Confusion, fear, disappointment… all of it- go in."

Now picture yourself walking that backpack over to Jesus.

Say: "This isn't mine to carry. You lead, I'll follow. I trust You with this, it's too heavy for me."

Then breathe.

This is where surrender becomes real not as a concept, but as a practice. There is strength in laying down what was never meant to live inside your body. Peace comes when you place your pain in the hands of the One who can actually carry it. You don't have to carry it anymore.

Jesus never wanted us to carry our burdens alone. Scripture is very clear on this. Remember this! God doesn't stand back and cheer us on. He upholds. He doesn't say He'll remove every burden immediately, He says He will sustain you while you release it. Not some of it. Not the manageable parts. All of it. Go to Him and rest!

OTHER ROOTS THAT SUSTAINED ME

God is my foundation, but in everyday life, it's people, responsibilities, and small, intentional practices that help me remain rooted.

My "Why"

There were days I wanted to give up. I'd look at my kids and remind myself: *They need a whole, not healed but healing version of me.* I wanted to break the cycle, not repeat it. I wanted them to know what emotional safety feels like because I didn't always have that growing up.

The divorce impacted my kids tremendously. As much as my life

　　　LEMON SEEDS

changed, so did theirs and quicker than any of us could process. That's why it became a priority that they saw me doing the work. I wanted them to know that healing was possible, even in the middle of hard times. That it's okay to not have it all together, it's not okay to stop trying.

By watching me do the work, they learned they could come to me with their own worries, fears, questions, and frustrations. I became the safe place I never had growing up.

When you find your why, you find your reason to keep going. When you forget your why, you risk losing yourself again.

Your "why" may not be a person. It could be a responsibility, a goal, or a version of yourself you're committed to becoming. Whoever—or what-ever—it is, make sure it carries enough emotional weight to keep you moving forward when things feel heavy and progress feels slow.

Ask yourself this: "Who would be impacted if you decided to stop show-ing up?"

ROUTINES THAT ROOTED ME

Let's be real, I'm human, just like you. Yes, I use my phone as an alarm clock, which is one of the worst habits, because here's what happens:

The alarm goes off, I hit snooze more than once, and I've already got:

- Five text messages (one that's got my blood pressure rising)

- Twenty emails

- Two missed calls

- A reminder for a sale I "can't miss"

- A long list of to-dos that start chasing me before my feet hit the floor

I realized I was starting my day in chaos by choice. When you start to heal, you start to crave peace in every area of your life. So, I started building simple routines that grounded me:

Morning quiet time. Even if I'm running late, I leave my blinds open on the second story. I wake up to sunshine, swaying trees, and flying birds. I whisper, "Thank You, God, for another day."

My daily prayer:

> *God, thank You for today. Use me as you see fit. Let me serve the people You've chosen for me. Protect me. Give me courage and wisdom. Help me recognize the opportunities you've placed in front of me, and allow me to steward them well.*
>
> *In Jesus' name, Amen.*

A morning walk. After getting the kids ready, in my robe and with my messy bedhead, I walk my dogs. Sometimes I tune into the sounds of nature, other times I listen to worship music or a prayer.

Journaling. With everything racing through my mind, deadlines, calls, clients, co-parenting, events I take a few moments to release my thoughts on paper. It clears my head and calms my spirit.

Intentions with the kids. On the way to school, we either blast worship music or their favorite songs. When we hit a specific stop-light, one of us calls out, *"What's your intention for the day?"* Each of us shares. It's simple, but sacred.

These small rhythms became holy. They reminded me: I'm safe now. I don't have to hustle through this season. I can live a slower, more peaceful, even messy life, and still enjoy the moments I've been given.

SAFE PEOPLE

Healing teaches you discernment. Discernment is one of the gifts of the Holy Spirit—the ability to recognize what is from God and what is not, when to open your heart and when to protect it. Over time, I learned a difficult but freeing truth: not everyone deserves access to you.

Some people genuinely want to support you. Others are simply curious about your wounds. I became intentional about who I allowed to speak into my life and who I chose to walk closely with. I didn't want people who only wanted to talk about everything that was wrong or gossip about my pain. I wanted people who were willing to sit with me and pray. People who didn't shrink from my pain, but made room for it. People who reminded me of the truth when I forgot it.

Many people don't even realize it, but they're more comfortable having a front-row seat to your struggle than helping you rise out of it. Chaos can feel familiar. Drama can feel bonding. But neither is healing.

Jesus never asked us to give everyone equal access to our lives. He taught discernment, not suspicion—wisdom, not isolation. Scripture reminds us to look at fruit, not intention. Some people may care about you deeply and still not be safe to walk closely with you in certain seasons. Even Jesus loved people without entrusting Himself to them. Guarding your heart isn't a lack of love; it's an act of stewardship. Safe people bring peace, clarity, and truth. They respect boundaries, don't rush your process, and don't require you to betray yourself to stay connected.

My sister and I, both walking through our own struggles, used to call each other nearly every morning just to vent. We would unload everything that offended us or left us hurt, then wish each other a good day. It became routine. While it felt relieving in the moment, we eventually realized something important, we were giving too much energy to things that didn't deserve that much power.

So we made a choice. We decided to talk about the beauty in life more than the chaos. To refocus on what was real, not just what was loud.

You don't need a crowd to affirm everything that's going wrong in your life. You need a few well-intentioned, emotionally healthy people who leave you feeling strengthened, grounded, and encouraged to keep moving forward.

THE FUTURE ME

There are days where I feel completely overwhelmed. Days I want to throw in the towel. These days I don't want to deal with any of it.

Then I remember her. The woman waiting for me on the other side of this.

She is steady.
Healed.
Whole.
With boundaries.
Walking in joy.
Without pretending.

When I'm tempted to slip back into old habits or give into the weight of life, I anchor myself to her, the *future me*. The woman I'm becoming. Even when I can't see her clearly, I keep walking toward her.

Because she's not just a dream. She's the promise I'm building.

SEED FOR THOUGHT

Let yourself build slowly. Let yourself start again. Let yourself be held. You are not behind. You are becoming.

"And the God of all grace… will Himself restore you and make you strong, firm and steadfast."

1 Peter 5:10

Eight

THE POWER OF BELIEF

Belief is a force more powerful than we often realize. It's what carries us when nothing else can. It's the quiet voice inside that whispers, *"Maybe I can,"* and the loud roar that declares, *"Watch me."*

I didn't always understand the power of belief, especially not when I was at rock bottom. When you're surrounded by loss, betrayal, and disappointment, it's hard to believe in anything. In healing. In the future. In yourself.

There were seasons where I didn't believe I'd ever smile again without faking it. Moments where I didn't believe I was worthy of love, peace, or joy. Nights where I questioned if God knew I still existed.

But belief, true, soul-deep belief isn't just something you feel. It's something you choose.

You choose it on the days you don't see a way forward. You choose it when the odds are stacked against you. You choose it when everything in you says quit, but your spirit whispers, *keep going.* I had to learn how to believe again, piece by piece. I want to help you do the same.

LOOKING BACK TO MOVE FORWARD

It's hard to be in a painful moment and hold onto the belief that a better day will come. When your heart is shattered, when the silence in your room feels louder than anything you've ever heard, belief feels impossible.

Deep inside, we know nothing lasts forever. Even in our lowest moments, there's a whisper faint but persistent that says, *"You won't always feel this way."*

For me, belief wasn't built from reading inspirational quotes or listening to motivational speeches. It was built by looking back.

Let's do that together.

Think of a moment in your life that brought you to your knees. Maybe it was a breakup. A job loss. A betrayal. A fight that changed everything.

Go there in your mind not to stay, to reflect.

- What did you feel in that moment? Defeated? Alone? Scared? Numb?
- What emotion rose up? Rage? Shame? Grief?
- Then, this is important, how did you react?
- Did you cry? Shut down? Numb out? Pretend everything was fine?

I know this part is uncomfortable. I want you to stay with it. Because now, look at everything that's happened since.

Ask yourself:

- Has your life been devastated ever since?

- Have you smiled since then?

- Laughed?

- Found joy in moments?

- Do you remember the moment when that pain no longer defined you?

That's belief in action.

We think belief is something magical or motivational. Sometimes, belief is just the choice to keep going. One breath. One step. One decision at a time. Until one day, you realize, you made it through what once felt impossible. That's the power of belief.

THE WAITING SEASON: WHERE BELIEF IS BUILT

When I decided to leave my marriage, I didn't find myself in this newly found life that I was proud of. Actually it was quite the opposite, yet exactly what I needed. I had moved back into my parents house, living in one room on a queen bed with my two kids. I closed my business, and honestly I felt so far from where I wanted to be, yet so close to what God was calling me to become.

I called it a setback. But God? He called it a setup.

At the time, I didn't see that. I saw a grown woman. A mother. A former business owner. Sleeping in one room with my kids on a queen-size bed. No privacy. No peace. Just survival mode. All I could feel was failure. I compared the teenage version of myself to the version of me I used to be. I resented that the vision I had once declared so boldly now felt like a lie.

When you're in the *waiting season*, in between the life you lost and the one you haven't reached yet it's easy to focus on everything that's missing.

Belief? It's born in that in-between.

I didn't have the answers. I didn't have a strategy. I didn't even have peace. I did have belief, the kind that grows in the dark. The kind that whispers *"God's not finished"* even when everything around you says it's over.

That season wasn't punishment, it was preparation. That room became my altar. My prayers got honest. My faith got raw. Little by little, I started to rise again.

Belief is what made me get up again and say *Okay Nadine, let's do this one more time.* It's what made me dream again, this time with God as my CEO.

Now, I look around at the life I've rebuilt, the thriving business, the home I love, the clients I serve, the friends I have, and I think of that woman who once felt invisible in her parents' house.

She didn't see this version of me, but she believed anyway. That kind of belief. It doesn't wait for proof. It prepares you for what's next.

Write this down: "If it doesn't make sense yet, then God's not done with it." If it's still cloudy, then He's still working. That means there's more to come. Your job? Is to believe.

BELIEF THAT BECOMES ACTION

Belief isn't just something you feel, it's something you move with. It becomes the lens you use when everything still looks blurry. It's the fuel behind every shaky yes. Every attempt to show up again. Every moment you speak life into a vision no one else sees yet. I didn't rebuild my life with a step-by-step plan.

 LEMON SEEDS

Most of the biggest shifts in my life started with me having no idea how it would turn out.

We're taught to plan everything. Just like when you apply for a business loan, you submit a perfect plan with goals, budgets, projections. No one asks: What's your plan when it all goes wrong? Life doesn't care about your 12-point pitch deck in Times New Roman.

Life *happens*. Belief is what carries you when it does. You can say, *This is happening to me.* Or you can choose the posture of belief and say, *This is happening for me.*

BELIEF IN ACTION: THE CHEAT CODE

I've become detached from outcomes, not because I don't care, but because I've learned to trust that everything will unfold exactly as it should.

When I assume something won't work, I'm telling God I don't believe He can make it work, and He gives me exactly what I asked for: nothing.

When I walk into a room with the belief that *"Even if it doesn't go my way, I'm still going to be blessed,"* God shows up and uses me as I'm meant to be used.

That's it. That's the cheat code. I needed to believe that everything was working for me.

How do we change our story?

Belief-Building Exercise: Reverse the Lie

We don't change the way we show up by forcing optimism or pretending fear doesn't exist. What shapes us is repetition, thoughts we return to, assumptions we make, and narratives we allow to take root. Over time, those patterns become the lens through which we see God, ourselves, and what we expect from life.

If we don't interrupt those patterns intentionally, they quietly become our default.

Grab some sticky notes, index cards, or colored paper.

Then, take a blank sheet of paper and write down every limiting belief that's been living inside your mind. Be honest.

Some examples:

- "I'll never be successful."

- "I'm not lovable."

- "I don't matter."

- "No one supports me."

- "I'll never get ahead."

Get raw. The first time I did this, I listed *99* negative beliefs I was carrying.

With those sticky notes, write a truth for every lie (negative belief) you wrote.

If you wrote: *"I'm not lovable,"* your sticky note says: *"I am deeply loved by those around me."*

If you wrote: *"I live an unfulfilled life,"* your sticky says: *"I am walking in purpose."*

Put these sticky notes somewhere you'll see them every day. I placed mine around my mirror, so every day while I get ready, I see my truth reflected back at me.

 LEMON SEEDS

Here's what will happen:

The more you see it, the more you believe it. The more you believe it, the more you create it. The more you create it, the more it becomes your reality.

I now do this every 90 days. Sometimes I focus on money. Sometimes on healing. Sometimes relationships. Whatever I want to grow in, I write the belief first.

Then I watch God water it.

If you want to get even deeper into this exercise and give God the room he deserves. When you are writing out your beliefs, find a scripture to pair it with!

SEED FOR THOUGHT

Belief isn't about ignoring reality, it's about deciding that your current season doesn't get to define your entire life.

It's about choosing to trust God, even when you don't feel Him. It's about speaking the truth, especially when your circumstances are shouting lies It's about acting in faith even when you don't see the fruit yet.

You're not just believing *for* something, you're believing *through* something. You already have everything you need to become who you were born to be.

The work now? Believe it.

"Everything is possible for one who believes."

Mark 9:23

~ Nine ~

CONNECTING THE DOTS

WHEN EVERYTHING FINALLY MAKES SENSE

There's a sacred moment that happens in healing, the kind that doesn't make a sound, but shifts something in your spirit forever. It's the moment you stop asking, *"Why did this happen to me?"* Instead, you whisper, *"This is what it was for."*

That moment came for me in 2024.

I was 35 years old, a single mother of two, starting a new business. For the first time in my life, I wasn't driven by chaos or scarcity. I wasn't praying for the storm to pass, I was standing in the calm after it, realizing just how much the storm had changed me.

What surprised me most wasn't the relief, it was the clarity. Calm didn't mean everything was perfect. It meant my nervous system was no longer braced for impact. I wasn't scanning for what might go wrong. I wasn't budgeting my hope. For the first time, peace wasn't something I was chasing; it was something I was standing in.

THE FINANCIAL STORM I NEEDED

Finances had always been a constant thread of anxiety woven through my life, not because I didn't believe I could make money, but because the environments I had been part of treated money like a scarce, elusive thing.

As a kid, I heard the same phrase on loop: *"We don't have money for that."* As a young adult, I rebelled. I spent freely, recklessly, because I craved the feeling of abundance, even if it was an illusion.

When I got married and had kids, money became a pressure cooker. Every conversation about it was tense. The energy shifted the moment finances were brought up. I learned to avoid it, to make miracles out of overdrafts, to perform emotional gymnastics just to maintain the peace.

Even when I opened my café, when we were bleeding more money than we were bringing in, I didn't panic. I pivoted. I stayed up late brainstorming new menu items, created events to drive foot traffic, kept showing up. The idea of letting money stop me from living my dream felt like death.

Deep down, I was still tethered to fear. I just masked it with hustle.

A PRAYER THAT CHANGED EVERYTHING

Going back to the prayer that I prayed right before my life completely shifted,

I said, *"God, if something in my life is holding me back, or isn't supposed to be part of my story, I give You full control. Remove it from me abruptly if You have to because then I'll know it's Your hand, not just chaos. God, I don't even know exactly what it is. I just know I feel stuck. I know You are guiding me, but right now it feels like we've stopped walking. So please, cleanse my life of what's not aligned with You. Strip away what's no longer meant to stay. And guide me boldly and clearly into the life You've destined for me."*

What followed was a dismantling I didn't expect.

The very next day, I heard the Holy Spirit clearly whisper:
"File for bankruptcy."

I argued at first. *Was there another way? Couldn't I just work harder? Maybe I could fix it another way…*

The whisper came again, firmer this time:
"File for bankruptcy."

What made this so difficult wasn't the paperwork or the process, it was the identity death. Filing felt like admitting defeat in a world that equates worth with success. It forced me to confront a question I had avoided for years: Was I willing to obey God even if it made me look like I failed?

So I did. The moment I followed through, the same "life partner" who supported the decision turned on me, calling me a failure, a loser. The verbal daggers hurt. I knew I had been obedient. That had to be enough.

What I didn't know then was that I wasn't just filing bankruptcy on debt, I was filing bankruptcy on my old life.

Within months, I was filing for divorce, too.

WHAT FELT LIKE THE END WAS JUST THE EXODUS

I call it my *40 days in the desert.* Except it was closer to two years.

There were doors I had to close. People I had to walk away from. Beliefs I had to unlearn. My ego screamed. My heart broke. My spirit? My spirit knew I was walking toward something bigger than I could understand.

In 2024, something clicked. I was living in provision, not luxury, not over-flow, but peace. That was richer than any paycheck.

The conversation about money didn't stress me anymore. I could talk about it without that tightness in my chest. I wasn't waiting for the other shoe to drop, I was grounded. For the first time, I didn't need proof to know everything would be taken care of. I *knew*.

As I sat in prayer one night, preparing to write this book, I heard it again:

"Now you understand. This is why it all happened."

I had to go through debt to find freedom.
I had to lose the support of someone who no longer aligned with my purpose. I had to experience having *nothing* to realize what it meant to have *peace*. I had to lose the first business to make room for the one that was aligned.

Nothing was wasted. Nothing was random. Every moment had been a setup for this exact one.

I used to think God's faithfulness meant protection from loss. Now I understand it as redemption through loss. He didn't spare me from the unraveling, He repurposed it. What I called setbacks were actually cor-rections. What I called delays were recalibrations. Looking back, I can see that God wasn't removing things from me, He was removing things for me.

A DIVINE DELAY

There's another moment that proved this to me. It was so specific, I couldn't chalk it up to coincidence.

Back in 2018, I met Jeannine, we were both in totally different places of life. I was just starting my health and wellness business and was facing di-

   LEMON SEEDS

vorce at the time (don't judge me, I was committed to keeping my family together) and she invited me to brunch as she wanted to start her wellness journey. Random. Unscripted. She talked to me about real estate. While I was intrigued by her success, I was so into what I was doing and truth be told I just wanted to sell her my wellness plan. We took a picture at the end of brunch in front of the restaurant and I posted it on my social media.

God knew.

He knew I was going to reconcile my marriage. He knew I wasn't ready. He knew I still had some desert walking to do. So, He delayed the opportunity.

Fast forward to 2023. The day after mediation from my divorce and the day I prayed my third strongest prayer. With my Bible in my hand hovering over it with tears streaming down my face I prayed.

> *"God, I have a been obedient through this process and it has been so painful I have cried until there were no more tears to cry, I have held my tongue when I wanted to bring everyone down with my pain, I am at rock bottom God and I am so ready for what is to come next, so please God if you feel that I am ready too please put what is next in front me.*
>
> *In Jesus Name Amen."*

The very next day Jeannine called me with a business proposal. Same person. Same opportunity. A completely different version of me.

It hit me like a divine download:

"This couldn't have happened a moment sooner."

The opportunity didn't change, I did. The delay wasn't about timing; it was about formation. God wasn't withholding the door; He was strengthening who would walk through it. Some opportunities require a version of you that haven't been built yet.

That's how I know now: delays are not denials. They are divine strategies.

Reflection: When the Dots Begin to Connect

I believe God gives us these moments as gifts, not just so we can understand the past, so we can trust Him more deeply in the future. These full-circle moments aren't just stories to reflect on, they're proof.

Proof that obedience bears fruit.
Proof that surrender creates space.
Proof that God wastes *nothing*.

So if you're still in the middle, if the dots don't make sense yet, hold on. Because one day soon, you'll whisper it too: "This is what it was for."

SEED FOR THOUGHT

If you're somewhere in-between, not who you used to be, but not yet who you're becoming, please hear me: God is not done. The dots won't always connect while you're walking. Sometimes they only make sense when you look back. Just because you can't see the picture yet doesn't mean God isn't painting it.

**"In their hearts humans plan their course,
but the Lord establishes their steps."**

Proverbs 16:9

     LEMON SEEDS

~ Ten ~

FINDING JOY

The definition of joy according to Webster's Dictionary is:

Joy (noun):
A deep, abiding sense of peace, contentment, and well-being that exists regardless of circumstances.

The biblical definition of joy? It's even richer. Joy is described in Galatians 5:22 as a fruit of the Spirit, a *supernatural gladness* that comes from knowing, trusting, and walking with Jesus Christ. It's not situational. It's not self-manufactured. It's spiritual. It's not something we hustle to achieve; it's something we receive when we are deeply rooted in Him.

It's funny how often we hear people say, *"I just want to be happy."* It's the anthem of our generation, the goal we're all told to chase.

We scroll past photos of smiling faces, lavish vacations, career milestones, baby announcements, and highlight reels, and we think: *They must be so happy.* We associate happiness with success, fulfillment, even worthiness. For many years, I chased happiness the same way. I believed that once I had the relationship, the business, the house, the balance in my bank account, then I'd feel it for sure. I'd finally arrived happy. I'd finally be okay.

The problem with happiness is that it's fragile. It's a feeling, an emotional high that is constantly shifting depending on our circumstances.

According to Webster, *happiness* is:

Happiness (noun):
A temporary emotional state characterized by pleasure, contentment, or satisfaction, often triggered by external circumstances or favorable outcomes.

The word that jumps out most to me is *temporary.*

Looking back, I've experienced happiness in many moments, starting a new business, celebrating birthdays, making memories with my kids and friends, seeing dreams come to life. I was genuinely happy. I smiled, I laughed, I felt the lightness of it. I'm grateful for every one of those moments.

However, I began to notice a pattern: happiness always had an expiration date.

It was tied to something external, something that could change. When that thing shifted or faded, so did my contentment. The emotion would come… and then it would go. I found myself constantly chasing the next burst of it. Like a high. Like a hit of something that never truly satisfies for long.

          LEMON SEEDS

That's when it hit me: *happiness is the ultimate scam of life.*

Everyone is chasing it. Books are written about it. Courses are sold for it. People build their entire lives around trying to keep it. Yet… no one really knows how to make it stay. Because it wasn't meant to.

I remember the moment I caught onto the scheme.

From the outside, my life looked amazing. I had the smile, the schedule, the photos, the progress. My kids were healthy. My calendar was full. People looked at my life and saw *success*. Behind closed doors? I was tired. Empty. I was performing through my pain, carrying the weight of everything I had built, wondering why none of it made me feel whole.

That's when I realized: *I didn't need more happy moments. I needed something deeper.*

One day, a close friend and mentor looked me in the eye and asked, "Do you have joy?"

Without thinking, I said, "Of course I do." Her question pierced deeper than my surface-level response. She wasn't asking if I had happy days. She was asking if I had something unshakable inside of me, something sacred. I couldn't stop thinking about it. That night, I went home and looked up the definition of joy.

That's when I understood: Joy is something entirely different from happiness.

It's not a quick fix. It's not triggered by compliments, paydays, or perfect photos. Joy is rooted. It's a presence planted deep within your spirit, so even when life doesn't go as planned, you still have peace. You still have strength. You still have Jesus.

Joy is what lets you cry over a loss and still believe there's hope. Joy is what keeps you grounded when everything around you is uncertain. Joy is what lets you wake up and whisper, "Thank You, Lord," even when nothing feels certain.

Where happiness is loud, fleeting, and performance-driven, joy is quiet. Sacred. Eternal. It's born in surrender. It grows in gratitude. It is sustained only by grace.

That question, *"Do you have joy?"* unlocked something inside me. I realized in that moment: I didn't. Not fully.

I could think of a few times I'd felt it, the births of my children being the most vivid, but on a day-to-day basis, joy wasn't what was holding me together. My strength came from striving. From control. From adrenaline and grit. Not from rest. Not from surrender. Not from joy.

Even though I couldn't say joy lived inside of me yet, something shifted in that moment. Because now, I knew there was a deeper, more intimate, more spiritual way to live, a kind of peace that didn't depend on everything going right. A kind of lightness that didn't fade when the world got heavy.

I knew I wanted it. I didn't just want to be happy. I wanted to be rooted. I wanted joy.

That pursuit began to separate me from everything in my life that was built on temporary emotions, including my marriage.

I remember vividly, during the later years of my marriage, my husband would often say, *"I'm just not happy."*

LEMON SEEDS

At first, I took those words personally. I thought maybe I wasn't doing enough. Maybe I wasn't enough. I tried to overcompensate, by doing the things I knew he enjoyed, saying yes to everything, trying to keep the peace, pouring from an already-empty cup. I thought if I just gave more, tried harder, smiled longer, I could help him find what he was missing.

Over time, I realized something that changed me forever:

I wasn't responsible for his happiness.

You hear the phrase all the time: *"Happy spouse, happy house."*

That kind of thinking can become dangerous when we start believing we are the source of someone else's joy, or worse, that they are the source of ours.

Eventually, I had to come to terms with a truth that not everyone is ready to hear:
We are each individually responsible for our own happiness, fulfillment, and healing.

No partner, no title, no child, no success can do the inner work for you. It's yours to do.

I was doing that work, every single day. I was praying, growing, healing, seeking peace, searching for purpose, letting go of what no longer served me. I was becoming a woman with joy in her heart.

The more I grew, the more the distance between us became undeniable. Because when one person evolves and the other stays the same, or worse, resents your growth it creates a tension that can't be ignored.

I remember sharing this with him once. I said something like, *"Maybe happiness isn't something I can give you. Maybe it's something you have to build for yourself."*

He didn't like that answer. Not one bit. Deep down, I knew it was true. I think that was the moment we truly began to part ways. It was a soul-level recognition that we were walking two very different paths.

You see, when you start walking toward wholeness, when you start choosing joy, doing the deep healing work, and anchoring your life in something bigger than external success you *will* be separated from your norm.

It's not punishment. It's alignment.

God will begin to gently (and sometimes not so gently) peel away anything that can't come with you into your next season. People. Patterns. Mindsets. Even marriages. Though it may feel painful, it's actually one of the greatest acts of love He can show you.

Your purpose can't thrive where your peace is constantly sacrificed. Real joy? It cannot exist in a place where your spirit is always shrinking just to keep the peace.

As I kept growing, I started to see clearly: I wasn't being selfish by prioritizing my inner joy. I was finally honoring the truth that God had placed within me.
In doing so, I began to attract more peace, more clarity, more purpose… even if it meant letting go of what I thought my life was supposed to look like.

I had once believed that staying in a relationship at all costs was strength. Now I understand, sometimes the strongest thing you can do is walk away when staying means abandoning yourself.

That was the beginning of true joy for me. Not the fleeting kind. Not the kind that needs perfect days to exist. It was the sacred, God-given joy that rises from a soul in alignment with truth, with peace, and with Him.

     LEMON SEEDS

Alignment is when your internal world, your thoughts, values, spirit, and actions, match the external life you're living. It's when you stop living for the applause and start living for the assignment.

I knew I had reached a misalignment when everything around me looked like success, but I was spiritually tired, emotionally empty, and constantly searching for more.

JOY BRINGS ALIGNMENT

Here's the truth I came to realize:
When you find true joy, you naturally fall into alignment.

Because joy is the evidence that your soul is in the right place. Not striving, not performing, not proving, but resting.

When Jesus said, *"so that My joy may be in you and your joy may be complete,"* *John 15:11,* He was showing us the blueprint for a life of alignment.

Joy isn't just an emotion. It's an indicator.
A spiritual signpost that says:
"You're connected. You're covered. You're where you need to be."

Joy doesn't scream. It doesn't demand attention. When it's present, you know, you feel that deep, steady peace that anchors you, even when life is uncertain.

Alignment happens when your spirit, your mind, and your actions all point in the same direction: toward Jesus.

Here's the beautiful part:
When you're aligned with Him, you're no longer forcing things to work. You're not begging people to understand you. You're not over-explaining, overcompensating, or overthinking. You're just being.

You're operating from overflow, not obligation. You're trusting more than you're controlling. You're flowing, not forcing.

Joy brings clarity. It sharpens your discernment. It silences the noise. It gives you the courage to release anything that no longer fits the version of you God is calling forward.

Anything that costs you your joy, your alignment… is too expensive.

GRATITUDE: THE GATEWAY TO JOY

I didn't always understand how closely joy and gratitude were connected. In fact, for a long time, I thought joy was the *reward* at the end of the journey, and gratitude was just a nice thing you did when things went well.

When I found myself in the trenches, navigating heartbreak, loss, and uncertainty I realized something profound: gratitude isn't a response to joy… it's the foundation of it.

When life broke me open, and I had nothing but faith to stand on, I started practicing something small yet powerful: I would speak thanks out loud, even when I didn't feel thankful.

I would whisper,
"Thank You for the breath in my lungs."
"Thank You for my children's laughter."
"Thank You that I'm still here."
"Thank You that You're still with me."

At first, it felt mechanical. Like I was trying to convince myself of something that hadn't yet arrived. Day by day, I felt a shift. Not in my circumstances, those took time, but in *me*.

        LEMON SEEDS

Gratitude softened the edges of my pain.

Gratitude made room for peace.

Gratitude *welcomed* joy in.

It wasn't the kind of joy that needed everything to be perfect. It was the kind that whispered: Even here, even now, even with all that hurts… I am held.

That's when I learned this unshakeable truth:

> You don't wait for joy to come before you give thanks
>
> You give thanks, and joy comes in the door.

There were days when the only thing I could thank God for was strength to get through the day. That was enough. Gratitude doesn't require a list of wins; it only asks for a willing heart.

I learned to give thanks in *becoming*, before the healing was complete, before the blessings were visible, before the peace was fully felt.

Gratitude became my daily declaration that I was still aligned with God's goodness, even when I couldn't see the full picture yet. In that posture, open hands, surrendered heart, joy found me.

HOW JOY SHOWS UP NOW

Joy used to feel like a goal I couldn't quite reach. A concept reserved for people with easier stories or smoother paths. Now, after the losses, the letting go, the rebuilding, I realize: joy was never out of reach… I just didn't know where to look.

Today, joy shows up in the smallest, most sacred ways.

It shows up in the morning light hitting my kitchen table while my kids eat breakfast. In the sound of my kids' voice saying, "I love you, mom," when I least expect it. In the quiet mornings I get to myself before the house wakes up. In the confidence I feel walking into a room knowing I'm in alignment with purpose, with peace, with Jesus.

Joy shows up in the calm I carry, even when plans fall apart. It shows up in how I trust now, not with tight fists, with open hands. It shows up in the way I no longer hustle for worth or wait for someone else to validate my path.

Joy isn't loud. It's not performative. It's not made for the highlight reel. Joy is that still, steady knowing deep in my bones that I am good. I am covered. I am on purpose.

It shows up when I take a walk and thank God just for being alive. It shows up when I don't have the answers but I feel held anyway. It shows up when I say "no" without guilt. When I rest. When I laugh. When I trust.

Perhaps most beautifully, it shows up when I can love others without fear, expectation, or depletion, because I'm no longer loving from lack. I'm loving from a cup that overflows.

Joy is no longer something I seek. It's something I *steward*. It lives in me now, because I made space for it.

PROTECTING MY JOY

After all I've been through, losing what I thought was forever, rebuilding from nothing, and walking through the wilderness with only faith to hold on to, I don't let just *anything* or *anyone* have access to me anymore.

Not out of pride.

    Not out of ego.

        But out of reverence.

    LEMON SEEDS

Because what God and I have built inside of me? It's *holy.*

Protecting my joy now means being *clear and unapologetic* about my boundaries. It means saying no, even when it disappoints people, if it costs me peace. It means not over-explaining myself to people who are committed to misunderstanding me. It means recognizing when someone's energy is not aligned with the life I'm building and not trying to force it to fit.

I've learned that discernment is a spiritual gift. Part of protecting your joy is listening when your spirit says, "This is not for you." I don't entertain relationships that require me to abandon myself to keep them. I don't overextend just to prove I'm good enough.

Protecting my joy is now part of how I honor God. Because when He delivers you out of darkness, you don't go back and play in the shadows. Protecting it doesn't mean living a guarded life. It means living a *rooted* one.

Rooted in Him.
 Rooted in truth.
  Rooted in what's real.

I now ask: Does this conversation, this relationship, this opportunity bring me closer to the woman I'm becoming, or pull me back into survival mode?

Joy is a gift. A treasure. A spiritual inheritance. Now that I've found it, I guard it fiercely, not out of fear, but from a place of *freedom.*

JESUS: THE ANCHOR OF MY JOY

The world changes. People leave. Plans fall apart. Money comes and goes.

But Jesus? He stays.

In John 15:11, Jesus says:

"I have told you this so that my joy may be in you and that your joy may be complete."

He wasn't talking about surface-level happiness. He wasn't promising perfect circumstances. He was offering something deeper, His joy. A joy that is *complete, unshakable,* and *not of this world.*

When I was walking through the darkest valleys of my life, bankruptcy, divorce, starting over from scratch. Joy wasn't something I could pretend to have. I wasn't chasing highs anymore. I was in survival mode. I was face down in prayer, desperate for direction, trying to breathe through the weight of it all.

T*hat* is where Jesus met me. Not on the mountaintop. Not in the wins. But in the wilderness. He didn't just comfort me. He *filled* me.

Not with fleeting relief. With something deeper: His presence. His peace. His joy.

That's how I know it's real. Because it didn't show up when life was easy. It showed up when I had nothing left but Him.

Joy doesn't come from everything going right. It comes from knowing the One who is right beside you, no matter what goes wrong.

Every moment I've spent with Him, whether in stillness, in worship, in weeping. He has become a wellspring for my soul. He steadied me when I couldn't stand. He reminded me who I was when I forgot. He whispered, *"My joy is in you. Let it be your strength."*

So now, I don't chase joy. I abide in it, because I abide in *Him.*

TAKE ROOT: CULTIVATING JOY + ALIGNMENT

This week, take intentional time to reflect and realign. Get quiet with yourself and with Jesus. Grab a journal and work through the following:

- **Identify what feels out of alignment.**
  What areas of your life feel heavy, forced, or disconnected?
  Is there anything you're doing just to keep up an image, maintain a role, or meet others' expectations?

- **Write out where you've been chasing happiness.**
  Where have you been seeking validation, comfort, or satisfaction from temporary things?
  What does that cycle of chasing feel like in your body and spirit?

- **Describe what true joy would look like for you.**
  What would life feel like if you were rooted in joy instead of reaching for happiness?
  How would your mornings change? Your relationships? Your thoughts?

- **Ask Jesus to reveal what needs to go so joy can grow.**
  Pray this:
  "Jesus, show me what I've been holding onto that's been blocking my joy.
  I surrender my idea of 'happy' for the fullness of who You are.
  Align me with what's real, what's right, and what's ready for me.
  Make joy my default, not just my desire."

- **Make one joyful decision this week.**
  It could be choosing rest instead of rushing, honesty instead of hiding, silence instead of striving, or grace instead of guilt.
  Whatever it is, choose the thing that aligns you, not the thing that appeases others.

SEED FOR THOUGHT

I now understand—joy is the foundation.

Joy is what allows you to keep building even when everything feels uncertain. Joy is what steadies your heart when the winds of life blow harder than expected. Joy is the whisper of God that says, *"I am with you, even here."*

Peel those layers back, and you'll find it again. Joy doesn't come from what you achieve. It comes from who you align with.

**"Do not grieve, for the joy of the
Lord is your strength."**

Nehemiah 8:10

Eleven

THE TRUE YOU

There's a moment in every healing journey when you realize you're no longer who you used to be, but you're not yet who you're becoming. You're somewhere in the middle. It's uncomfortable, sacred, and powerful all at once.

This is where the real work begins.

After being in a relationship and raising children since I was 18, I found myself single at 32. Suddenly, on the days my children weren't with me, I had time, time that was mine. So I filled it. I went out with friends. I danced the night away. I dated. I told myself I was making up for lost time. For the moments I felt I'd missed out on.

What I quickly came to realize was this: I hadn't missed out on much at all.

Growing up, I always said I'd be this fun, free-spirited girl forever. While that still rings true, it's true in a different way now. I no longer wanted my life to feel like a fast-moving roller coaster. That version of fun didn't feel like me anymore, it drained me. Meeting new people, sharing energy just to avoid feeling alone… it became exhausting.

When you go through loss, whether it's a relationship, identity, or dream you're often tempted to fill the void. The world will offer you a hundred ways to do it. If you sit in silence long enough, you'll begin to hear what truly fulfills you.

That still, small whisper began to speak louder. Don't go out tonight. Stay in. You'll be well rested for what I have planned for you tomorrow. I started noticing the people I surrounded myself with how they, too, were trying to fill something empty inside of them. It wasn't that I was better. I was just being obedient to the whisper that had started to sound more like a shout. I couldn't ignore it anymore.

Many of my kid-free days became what I call *cave days.* Days where the world went quiet and it was just me and the Holy Spirit. No little giggles echoing through the halls. No "Mom!" being shouted from the other room. Just silence and guidance.

When I made the decision to walk this journey of healing and to be spiritually led, I knew I would have to be different. It didn't happen overnight. It was slow. A gradual, undeniable transformation. Anytime I tried to go against what I felt God was telling me, it fell apart. The interest, the energy, the desire, gone. Every time I ignored the whisper, I regretted it.

I used to fear being alone. Now I treasure it. Because solitude helped me reconnect with God, and who He created me to be.

Friends and family would sometimes ask, "Are you okay? Are you de-

LEMON SEEDS

pressed?" I'd smile and reassure them, "I'm doing just fine." For the first time, I meant it.

Stepping outside of your normal circle to step into your own calling can feel lonely. I didn't have a tribe of women walking the beach with me, dreaming out loud about God's promises and how far we'd come. I had my immediate family, and a few I could call when needed. Even though I've always loved being social, I understood the solitude was part of the assignment.

What I discovered about myself during that time wasn't new. It had always been there. I just had to make space for it to awaken. That's true for you, too. You don't have to become someone else. You just have to *remember* who you are.

You may be asking: *Nadine, how do I know who the true me is? How do I find her again?*

Start here: If money, fear, criticism, and doubt were no longer factors, who would you be?

Go back to the last time you felt free to dream. For most of us, it was childhood. For me, it was playing teacher in my room with my stuffed animals. I'd line them up, hand out assignments, motivate them (okay, sometimes I yelled), and teach them about books I didn't even fully understand. I *loved* it. That little girl was already carrying a purpose.

It's no accident that now, after all I've walked through, I'm writing this book, teaching again, just in a different way.

I went to college, but I didn't major in psychology like I wanted to. The world told me that it wasn't practical. That it didn't pay. I studied business instead. I told myself the lie that a dream not approved by others wasn't worth pursuing. The calling was still there. It's always been there.

You see, finding yourself isn't about creating something new. It's about returning to what God planted in you from the beginning, before the heartbreak, before the pressure, before the titles.

For years, I was known for what I *did* for others: a wife, a mom, a business owner, a fixer, a peacemaker, the strong one. I wore every role like armor. Somewhere along the way… I forgot my name.

I forgot what it meant to check in with my own spirit. I forgot what made me laugh. I forgot how to be still without guilt. I forgot what it meant to belong to *me*.

That forgetting came at a cost. When you're disconnected from yourself, it becomes easy to accept a life that was never meant for you.

Even in business, I remember copying the habits of successful people, waking up at 5am, talking about the same trendy topics. Until I realized I was building a brand that didn't feel like mine. I was living for their approval, not my purpose.

God began to convict me: "If you're growing a life for them, give them your paycheck too."

That's when everything started to shift.

I started showing up differently. I stopped asking for permission. I stopped trying to shrink myself to fit into what others expected. I started being *loyal to my calling* more than I was to their comfort.

Finding yourself isn't about force. It's a gentle, sacred return.

It happens in the quiet mornings when you pray not just to be seen, but to *see* yourself again. It happens when you set boundaries, not just with people, but with your own patterns. It happens when you tell the truth, even when it shakes your voice. It happens when you choose rest, reflection, and radical honesty. Spiritually, it's a return to your Creator.

When I stopped performing and started surrendering, I began to embrace who God created me to be. Not perfect. Not polished. Purposeful.

Psalm 139:13-14 says: *"For You created my inmost being; You knit me together in my mother's womb. I praise You because I am fearfully and wonderfully made."*

I started meditating on that scripture daily. If God handcrafted me with intention, who am I to live like I'm not enough?

The world wants to define you by titles, by timelines, by trauma. Your soul was never meant to be reduced to a role. You are not your relationship status. You are not your bank account. You are not your mistakes. You are not just someone's something. You are a whole soul. With a purpose. With a voice. With a divine assignment.

When you start treating that truth as sacred, your whole life begins to shift. You walk differently. Think differently. Choose differently. Speak with more clarity. More confidence. More conviction. You stop waiting for the world to crown you, and you start walking in the truth that *you've already been chosen.*

Finding yourself isn't selfish. It's *sacred.*

The more you remember who you are, the more you reflect on the One who made you. That, my friend, is what freedom really feels like.

TAKE ROOT: COMING HOME TO YOU

I'm going to walk you through an exercise a good friend and my spiritual healer, Dr. Sandra Carter, has me do frequently.

1. Take your journal and find a quiet space.

2. Write a letter addressed to God. In this letter, release and forgive anything and everything you've stored inside of you. Think back as far and deep as you need to. For everything that surfaces, write: "God, I release…" or "God, I forgive…"

Name people. Name moments. Be specific. Pour it all out.

3. Place the letter in a bowl and burn it. Once it becomes ash, take it outside away from your home, and bury it. Walk away without looking back.

4. Go inside. Do some self-care. Like, washing your hair or paint your nails. Rest for the evening. Do this as often as you need.

5. Then, sit with yourself. This next part is from my own personal journaling practice:

Answer these questions honestly no filters, no fear:

- Who was I before the world told me who to be?

- What version of myself have I been pretending to be to stay accepted, liked, or safe?

- What dreams or desires keep resurfacing, even when I try to ignore them?

- What lights me up?

- Where in my life am I shrinking to make others comfortable?

- What does the truest, most aligned version of me feel like?

Then pray: "Lord, help me remember the person You created me to be. Strip away what doesn't belong to me. Remind me of what You placed in me from the beginning."

Now start taking small steps every day to live like that version of you is already here, because she is.

　　　LEMON SEEDS

SEED FOR THOUGHT

Finding yourself doesn't mean becoming someone new. It means shedding what was never yours and rising into the person you were always meant to be.

It's already in you. Let it lead.

> **"Put off your old self… and put on the new self, created to be like God in true righteousness and holiness."**
>
> **Ephesians 4:22–24**

Twelve

CREATING THE LIFE YOU LOVE

I've done it all. The vision boards. The late-night Pinterest scrolling. The five-year plans. The carefully written goals and ambitions, trying to decide what I wanted my life to look like.

I thought clarity would come from planning. I thought confidence would come once I could see it clearly enough.

After living through seasons that shattered me, losses I couldn't understand, pain that didn't fit neatly into a plan my trust in the future became fragile. I wanted a good life, but I was afraid to move toward it. Afraid that the moment things felt whole again, they'd fall apart.

So I stayed still.

Survival taught me how to endure, but it didn't teach me how to *choose*. And eventually, I realized something uncomfortable but true: staying stuck was safer than risking hope.

Until one day, I decided to move anyway.

THE MOUNTAINTOP MOMENT

There's a moment in Scripture where Moses stands before God, terrified of the assignment placed in front of him. He lists every reason he's not qualified. Every reason he can't do it. And instead of disqualifying him, God reassures him.

Not by explaining the plan, but by promising His presence.

That story matters because most of us don't hesitate to move forward because we lack vision. We hesitate because we're afraid we won't be held if we do.

I want you to have your own mountaintop moment.

Not the dramatic kind. The honest kind.

The moment you stand before God and say,

"I don't have what it takes. I don't know where to start. I'm scared to try again. But if this is what You're calling me to, I need You to lead me."

That moment even if it lasts only seconds creates permission. Permission to believe you're not crazy for wanting more. Permission to dream again. Permission to trust that what's inside you exists for a reason.

FROM SURVIVING TO CHOOSING

For many of us, survival is all we've known. Making it to the next moment while carrying grief, fear, and disappointment like a heavy backpack we never take off.

I had to relearn how to put that weight down. How to give it back to God. How to stop living as if I was still in crisis when the danger had already passed.

Creating a life you love doesn't begin with aesthetics or achievement. It begins with truth. The truth about what lights you up. The truth about what drains you. The truth about what you're tolerating. The truth about what you're called to.

Most people don't pause long enough to ask these questions. We're too busy checking boxes, proving worth, or staying afloat. But the life you love isn't something you stumble into. It's something you choose.

AWARENESS CHANGES EVERYTHING

A mentor once told me something I've never forgotten:

"You can create absolutely anything, but you have to decide how you're living."

You're either living consciously or by default.

Living consciously means you're aware of your thoughts, patterns, reactions, and choices. You notice what's driving you. You pause. You choose.

Living by default means those same things are still shaping your life, but without your participation. Old beliefs. Fear responses. Patterns you never intentionally chose. There is no in-between.

Every decision you make comes from awareness or autopilot. That's why healing matters; it interrupts the default settings. It gives you the space to notice *why* you respond the way you do, instead of letting the same scripts run on repeat.

When you become consciously aware, you start asking different questions:

"Is this thought even mine?"
"Am I reacting out of fear, or choosing from alignment?"

Once you see it, you can shift it.

LIVING AWAKE

Living consciously doesn't mean you'll always get it right. It means you're present enough to notice when something feels off and brave enough to correct it.

It looks like pausing before reacting.

Checking in with your spirit before committing.

Listening when something inside you says, *This isn't for you.*

It requires stillness. Reflection. Slowing down when the world tells you to speed up.

There are still moments when I react too quickly. Times I respond from old wounds instead of current truth. But now, I can sit with it. Reflect. Recognize that I felt unsafe and remind myself that I'm not living there anymore.

That's how you regain your power. You stop engaging in cycles you've outgrown. You walk away without explaining. You choose peace over proving.

ALIGNMENT OVER APPEARANCE

Loving your life isn't about constant excitement. It's about alignment. It's about waking up and feeling at home in your body, your schedule, your relationships, and your purpose.

You can have the dream career, the beautiful home, the picture-perfect life, and still feel empty if your spirit is out of sync with your steps.

Alignment doesn't come from performance. It comes from presence. God will always lead you back to the life He designed for you, but you have to be willing to release what He didn't.

That may mean letting go of roles you've outgrown. People-pleasing tendencies. A version of your life that looks good on the outside but no longer fits on the inside.

The life you love won't look like anyone else's. It will be unique to you. Rooted in your relationship with Jesus. Tailored to your soul.

Yes, it will require courage. And it will be worth it. Every boundary. Every honest yes. Every hard decision that brings you back to peace.

You are not behind.

You are not broken.

You are not too late.

The life you love is already waiting for you to choose it.

TAKE ROOT: BEGIN BUILDING

This week, be intentional.

Ask yourself:

- Where am I living by default instead of by design?

- What feels misaligned right now?

- What is one thing I can release?

- What is one thing I can choose differently?

- What belief am I ready to let go of?

Then take one step. It doesn't have to be big. Direction changes with movement.

Pray this:

"God, show me what's mine to carry in this season and what I need to lay down. Give me wisdom, courage, and trust as I choose alignment over fear."

SEED FOR THOUGHT

You don't create a life you love by copying someone else's blueprint. You create it by listening to the One who made you.

It won't always be easy.
It won't always be loud.
But it will be yours.

**"I will instruct you and teach you in
the way you should go; I will counsel
you with My loving eye on you."**

— Psalm 32:8

Thirteen

THE MEANING OF IT ALL

There comes a point in the journey after the tears, after the surrender, after the breaking and the rebuilding where you pause and ask yourself: *What was all of this for?*

Not from a place of pain. Not from a place of bitterness. From a place of clarity. Of reflection. Of peace.

At some point, survival is no longer the goal. The purpose is.

You begin to realize that every valley, every unanswered prayer, every sleepless night, and every redirection wasn't wasted. It was preparation. Divine, intentional, heaven-ordained preparation.

That's when the meaning begins to reveal itself.

MEANING DOESN'T COME ALL AT ONCE

Let me be honest, there were so many moments in my life where I sat in confusion. When I cried out, "God, what is this *for?*"

I didn't see the purpose in the pain. I didn't understand the assignment in the loss. I certainly didn't feel grateful for the waiting seasons that seemed to stretch longer than I thought I could endure.

Now? I look back, and I see the breadcrumbs. I see the connections. I see how it all aligned.

Meaning doesn't show up on demand. It arrives slowly, in layers, often long after the moment has passed. Sometimes in a conversation. Sometimes in a breakthrough. Sometimes in a quiet whisper that says, *This is what it was for.*

NOTHING WAS WASTED

Heartbreak? It softened me. Betrayal? It sharpened my discernment. Loneliness? It deepened my relationship with God. Waiting? It taught me patience and humility.

None of it was wasted.

That's the beautiful thing about divine healing. God doesn't just restore you, He redeems the *story.*

He takes the very things that broke you and uses them to build you. He takes what the enemy meant for evil and turns it for your good. Somehow, in a way only He can, He weaves your worst moments into your greatest testimony.

YOU WERE MADE FOR MORE

The deeper I go in this journey, the more I realize that we were never created just to *exist.* We were made to live fully. To love deeply. To create freely. To serve joyfully. To walk boldly in our purpose.

We were made for more than the pain. More than the grind. More than just surviving the day.

God didn't bring you this far just to leave you in limbo. He didn't rescue you just to watch you stay small. He brought you through *so you could go out and live differently.* So you could become a light to others walking through the same darkness.

Your life is not random. Your story is not an accident. You were created on purpose, for a purpose.

EVERYTHING COMES FULL CIRCLE

One of the most sacred things I've witnessed in my own life is the way things come full circle.

The moments that didn't make sense in the past suddenly connect to the blessings in the present. The things I once prayed for, but didn't receive are replaced with things I never could have imagined asking for.

Sometimes, you'll be brought back to the very place that broke you, but you'll return with healing in your hands. Sometimes, the people who once doubted you will witness the very calling they couldn't see in you. Sometimes, the door that once closed in your face will be reopened by your faith.

These full-circle moments aren't just for you, they're reminders of how intentional God truly is.

THE LEGACY IN THE LESSONS

I used to think legacy was about what I left behind. Now I know: it's about *how* I live while I'm here.

Every lesson I've learned is part of my legacy. Every child I raise with love and intention. Every woman I pour into. Every story I share. Every soul I get to help. Even though it's me that is doing it, it's His kingdom that I am building.

Legacy isn't just what the world remembers about you. It's what Heaven sees in you. It's the way you walk through life with courage, even when no one is watching. It's the way you choose love over fear, surrender over control, faith over striving.

The meaning of it all is this: To become the woman God created you to be, and to help others do the same.

To say yes when it's scary. To love when it's hard. To heal when it would be easier to stay bitter. To show up for yourself, for your children, for your calling.

To live your truth out loud.

WHAT HEALING HAS TAUGHT ME

Healing didn't make me perfect. It made me whole. It didn't erase my pain, it gave it a purpose. It didn't answer all of my questions, it taught me how to rest in the mystery. It didn't fix every relationship, it reconnected me to the One relationship that matters most. Healing didn't change who I am. It returned me to who I've always been. In return, I found the meaning.

The meaning of every valley. The meaning of every mountaintop. The meaning of every season in between.

WHAT WAS IT ALL FOR?

It was for the version of me writing this right now. The one who knows in her spirit that there is more. The one who is no longer content with surviving. The one who is finally ready to start living, *really* living.

It was for you. So you could hold this book in your hands and say: I'm not alone. I'm not too late. I'm not too broken. I'm just getting started.

It was all for this moment. This clarity. This courage. This choice. To rise. To heal. To become. To live.

You're Not Too Late, No Matter Your Age

If there's one lie I want to shatter in your mind before you close this book, it's this one:
That it's too late for you.
Too late to start over.
Too late to dream again.
Too late to find purpose, or joy, or love, or freedom.
Too late to be the version of you that God had in mind all along.

IT IS NOT TOO LATE.

I don't care if you're 35, 45, 55, or 75, you are *not* behind. Let me remind you of some names you might know:

- Vera Wang didn't design her first dress until she was 40.

- Colonel Sanders founded KFC at 65.

- Julia Child didn't debut her first cookbook until 50.

- Morgan Freeman became a household name after 52.

- Grandma Moses began painting in her late 70s.

- Joyce Meyer didn't step into full-time ministry until her 40s.

- Even Abraham and Sarah in the Bible received their promised child, Isaac, *long* after their youth had passed.

Because when God has called you to something, time bows to *His* timeline, not yours. Let that sink in.

Your purpose doesn't expire. Your gifts don't diminish with age. Your best days are *not* behind you just because the world told you they should've come sooner.

Some of us had to survive things first.
Some of us had to lose everything to find ourselves.
Some of us had to wander before we could come home to who we are.

You are right on time for the version of your life that *God* is writing.

The beautiful thing is: the older you get, the more wisdom you bring into the room. The more depth your story carries. The more impact you can make, not in spite of your age, but *because* of it.

Don't let your age be your excuse. Let it be your *evidence*.

You've lived. You've grown. You've endured. Now, you get to create something beautiful with all that you've learned.

This isn't your ending. This is your arrival. Everything, absolutely *everything*, was preparing you for this.

This Was the Beginning of Everything

There will come a moment maybe today, maybe tomorrow, maybe years from now when you will look at the very thing that once shattered you and say, *"That's the moment everything changed."*

Not because it felt good. Not because it was fair. Not because you would've chosen it. Because that pain didn't get the final word, *purpose* did. Not just any purpose. *Yours.*

You'll look at your heartbreak and realize it broke you open so God could pour in something new. You'll look at your confusion and see the crossroads that led you back to yourself. You'll look at your silence and realize

          LEMON SEEDS

it was in the quiet that you started to hear God more clearly.

This is how beauty is made from ashes. Not by pretending it didn't hurt. Not by minimizing what you've been through. By telling the truth, and still choosing to rise.

Your story doesn't end with what broke you. It begins with what you built after it. You may not have chosen the wound, but you *get to choose* the meaning you make from it. You get to say, "This didn't destroy me. It shaped me."

Let me say this clearly if you're still in the middle of the mess, I know how it feels to question if it'll ever get better. I know the ache of carrying something that no one else sees. I promise you: it won't always feel like this, but you have to choose that today is the day you make the step forward.

One day, this chapter you're in will be the one you tell with strength in your voice and peace in your heart. One day, your pain will be the permission someone else needs to believe in healing. One day, the same eyes that cried will sparkle with a joy you never thought was possible.

The meaning of it all isn't found in avoiding pain. It's found in allowing pain to *refine you*, not *define you.*

Let God use what was meant to break you as the very thing that built your foundation. Let your wounds become your wisdom. Let your scars become your sermon.

When you look back, may you smile not because it didn't hurt, but because *you made it count.*

SEED FOR THOUGHT

Just because life handed you lemons doesn't mean the story ends in bitterness.

Every sour season you've lived through planted something in you. What felt like endings were really lemon seeds small, bitter beginnings of something God was preparing to grow. You're not finished. You're becoming. And what's growing in you next will be beautiful.

"Though your beginning was small, yet your latter days will be very great."

Job 8:7

LEMON SEEDS

Dear Reader - Strong Heart - Beautiful Soul,

If these pages spoke to something deep inside you, if you found healing, hope, or even a tiny spark of courage, I want you to know: that matters. That means this book did exactly what it was meant to do.

Maybe… you're not the only one who needs it.

If someone you love is walking through pain, transition, or simply trying to find their way, I ask you—please share this book with them. Let this be a seed of hope in their life too.

We rise when we lift each other. We heal more deeply when we heal together. You never know how one story, one truth, can change someone's entire path.

If you'd like to stay connected, share your journey, or simply say hello, you can find me at **NadineMaldonado.com**.

Thank you for trusting me with your heart. You are seen, you are strong, and you are still growing.

With so much love and belief in your journey,

Nadine Maldonado ♡

NOTES

NOTES

NOTES

NOTES

NOTES

NOTES

NOTES

NOTES

NOTES